7/22

WORDS FOR SILENCE

WORDS FOR SILENCE

A Year of Contemplative Meditations

Gregory Fruehwirth, OJN
Preface by Archbishop Desmond Tutu

PARACLETE PRESS
BREWSTER, MASSACHUSETTS

Words for Silence: A Year of Contemplative Meditations

2008 First Printing

ISBN: 978-1-55725-601-0

Library of Congress Cataloging-in-Publication Data
Fruehwirth, Gregory.
  Words for silence : a year of contemplative meditations / Gregory Fruehwirth ; preface by Desmond Tutu.
    p. cm.
  Includes bibliographical references.
  ISBN 978-1-55725-601-0
  1. Church year meditations. I. Tutu, Desmond. II. Title.
  BV30.F78 2008
  242'.3--dc22
                              2008028204

10 9 8 7 6 5 4 3 2 1

Published by Paraclete Press
Brewster, Massachusetts
www.paracletepress.com

Printed in the United States of America

CONTENTS

◌PREFACE◌
by Archbishop Desmond Tutu

THE OBLATES AND ASSOCIATES of the Order of Julian of
Norwich are richly blessed, for we receive copies of the
chapter talks that Father Gregory, the Guardian of the Order,
delivers to the Members Regular, the nuns and monks of the
Order. How privileged we are to share these addresses with their
array of pearls of wisdom as we sit at the feet of someone so
profound yet so accessible.

The fact that talks primarily meant for monks and nuns are
shared with us who are "in the world" speaks eloquently of the
fact that the life of prayer, the contemplative life, is really for
all, not just for a select few, an elite ensconced in a monastery.
The exhortation that people pray without ceasing is meant not
just for an elite but is addressed to all of us who claim to be
followers of our Lord and Saviour Jesus Christ. We are meant to
emulate him, who was so conscious of the divine presence and
his unity with the divine source of all that he could in the fourth
Gospel declare, "the Father and I are one." We too should know
we are always in the presence of this God, even though we may
not always be aware of it because of our frenetic busyness; and
we have to pause, reassemble our scattered faculties, become
recollected as we savor the sanctity of the present moment, to
be still, for only so can we apprehend the one who said, "Be
still and know that I am God." This One who is to be found
most frequently, not in the spectacular but in the mundane, the
ordinary; not in the wind, not in the fire and the earthquake,
but in the still, small voice; in a little child lying in a manger, in

broken bread and a shared cup of wine. Every bit of ground we trample is actually holy ground.

Father Gregory in one set of talks encourages his audience to pay attention to the rhythms of their breathing. In that series he draws attention to how even our mealtimes might be occasion for growing in sanctity and in gratitude for God's provision by thinking, say, of the potato on one's plate, so bringing to mind the soil in which it was planted and nourished, the water, the air, the sunlight, the God who gives the increase, so we would not just gobble unmindfully, but be reflective and slow, which would be good for our digestion, too. In these ways we would be like Brother Lawrence, who found the clatter of the pots and pans in the kitchen as good in inducing holy thoughts as the liturgical acts in the sanctuary at the celebration of the Eucharist. Our real home is God, our natural environment is the divine—Teilhard de Chardin's *The Divine Milieu*—so that should be as natural for us as water for the fish and air for the bird, theophanic: the sacred could erupt anywhere at any time, every bush being potentially a burning bush. One of my confessors and spiritual counselors used to say, "Nothing is secular except sin."

We who lead so-called active lives in contrast to the contemplative (as if it could ever be just passive) have our work cut out to balance the Mary (the contemplative, still side) and the Martha aspects (the active, doing side).

I know that I would never have survived in our struggle against apartheid without the fairly substantial portions of my daily regimen devoted to the so-called spiritual—times of quiet, of meditation, praying the offices, celebrating the Eucharist, quiet days and retreats. Without these to nurture and sustain me I would have just collapsed. And there was ultimately no real dichotomy—it was the God one encountered in the quiet moments who demanded that we demonstrate our love for this God by our acts of love for neighbor, for how could we say we loved God whom we had not seen when we hated our brother/sister whom we had seen? "In as much as ye have done it to the least of these my sisters or brothers, ye have done it to me." The pattern had been established with our Lord after his baptism.

He did not luxuriate in the afterglow of that spiritual experience; no, the Spirit cast him into the fray with the devil. He had shown the pattern of engagement and disengagement, setting off alone to pray in the hills especially before some major item on his agenda, as for instance the call of the disciples, or going for replenishment after some demanding public work, as after the feeding of the five thousand.

And there were times when it seemed a divine pressure impelled me to do something totally unpremeditated, and yet once it happened it turned out to be so right. I was in retreat before my ordination as bishop when I thought God wanted me to write a letter to Prime Minister Vorster to warn him that black patience was running out. The letter virtually wrote itself. I sent it in May 1976. Mr. Vorster was disdainful. On June 16, 1976, the Soweto uprising happened. In 1989 black people demonstrated against the whites-only election, and in retaliation many of our people were killed. I broke down in my chapel in the Archbishop's residence in Cape Town after being told the latest casualties, and I emerged to say we must march. In September 1989 the largest march under apartheid happened when 30,000 people turned up—and that was the beginning of the end of apartheid.

We are always in God's presence. We are being urged to be more conscious of this and to be those who are still because we know that God is God.

+ Desmond M. Tutu
Archbishop Emeritus of Cape Town

INTRODUCTION

I N THE BENEDICTINE MONASTIC TRADITION it is customary for a chapter from the Rule of Saint Benedict to be read to the community each day. The abbot may then elect to give an explanation of the passage, guiding the community in its practice. This occasional address by the abbot, touching on the core meaning and practices of the monastery, has traditionally been called a "chapter talk."

My religious order, the Order of Julian of Norwich, is an Anglican order of contemplative monks and nuns in the Episcopal Church. While not strictly a Benedictine community, we have adopted a great deal from the Benedictine tradition, including weekly chapter talks by the superior aimed at providing consistent, long-term spiritual formation for the monks and nuns of the Order.

What follows is a selection of chapter talks from those I offered during the first four years of my term as guardian, or superior, of the community. These talks have ranged from the theological to the practical. Some have evoked the contemplative spirit, others have taught the theology behind a life of prayer, still others have offered instruction and encouragement in our daily practices. For this book, the talks have been arranged according to the seasons of the liturgical year. They can be read straight through or periodically. Each talk in *Words for Silence* has been substantially rewritten to apply to any person who is walking the contemplative path, who is seeking a more intimate union with God, or who is seeking to deepen her life of prayer.

Phrases such as "contemplative path" or "union with God" may be unclear to many who are first picking up this book. To others, such ideas may seem so exalted as to be beyond the reach of ordinary Christians. But this is not the case. Nothing is more ordinary, nothing is more natural, nothing more simple or humble than the authentic contemplative life that breathes in and out with God's Spirit through the trials and joys of a very ordinary day. Reaching such a state of complete naturalness and open joy in God does not require specialized learning or exalted spiritual experiences or a life in a monastery. It requires only a willingness to walk into daily life with the intention of living surrendered to God. As we become aware of the misguided desires and fears that drive us away from this intention, we let go of such things until we are stripped down to the natural, bare essence of our being, already enfolded in God's love.

Love is at the center of this process of becoming aware and letting go. The sense of being loved and cherished gives us the extraordinary freedom to see ourselves honestly, then to let go of the fears and delusions that usually shape our lives, and to greet the present moment as the place where we are already one with God. Unceasing prayer, long understood as the end of Christian and monastic life, is not an obsessive effort to pray a lot, but is an opening of our hearts and minds to the reality of God's love for us. It is a way of life shaped by that love. Simple, present, attuned, and surrendered, the contemplative spirit brings the kingdom of God to this world.

It will be helpful for many readers if I introduce the spiritual mothers and fathers who have preceded me in the Christian spiritual tradition. These great women and men have given me the concepts and language that have allowed me to take hold of my own vocation as a contemplative monk and wrestle with its hold on me, and their spirit is everywhere in these meditations.

First, St. Benedict's Rule has already been mentioned. Written in the early sixth century, this Rule has proved to be a touchstone for almost all of Western monastic life since then. Noted for its balance between work and communal prayer and meditation on Scripture, the genius of St. Benedict's Rule is its legislation of a way of life that is tempered enough to be truly livable and yet which leads nuns or monks, almost in spite of themselves, to become transparent to God.

Second, Blessed John Cassian is mentioned in many places in the pages that follow. Living in the fourth and fifth centuries, John Cassian traveled widely in the monastic circles of his day, receiving teaching firsthand from the great monastic fathers and mothers of the Egyptian and Syrian deserts. His two books, commonly known as *The Institutes* and *The Conferences*, brought the wisdom of the Desert Fathers and Mothers to the monastic traditions of the Eastern and Western Churches.

Third, St. John of the Cross, a Carmelite friar and mystic of sixteenth-century Spain, has been formative in my own spiritual journey and appears often in my reflections. John of the Cross's most important insight was that the trials and temptations that we undergo in the spiritual life—inner aridity, disturbing thoughts, negative moods—are often a result not of the absence of God, but of God's having drawn near. In one of John's favorite metaphors, the uncreated love of God, flowing into the soul, is like a flame kindled underneath a swampy log. Before the flame can consume the log and transform the wood into fire, it has to drive out of the log all that is unlike itself. Thus when God draws near to us, we are likely to experience not consolations or peace, but the driving up into conscious awareness all that seems most ungodly in us. We have to go backward to go forward, down to go up. A lifetime of wounds and suffering may come to the light of conscious awareness before they can be dispelled.

Finally, there is Blessed Julian of Norwich, whom I often call "Mother" Julian because she is the patron of my community and is my spiritual mother. She appears more often than any other writer in these meditations and has shaped my journey into God more than any other writer. Living in the fourteenth and fifteenth centuries, Mother Julian is known only because of her book *The Revelations of Divine Love*. This remarkable book is a combination of authentic mystical experience and twenty-plus years of astute theological reflection. Central to Julian's experience is the love of God and God's joy in us. The core of *The Revelations* is that God yearns to share his life of loving bliss with us. Julian reminds us again and again that at the heart of who we are, we are already united to God; our challenge is that in ordinary life we live in ways opposed to this deep union. Redemption happens when grace brings our outward life back into harmony with what is our deepest reality. The humanity of Jesus, particularly his suffering on the cross, is the means of our healing through which we are able to enter into God's love and joy. Our job is to learn how to cooperate with this working, and once again this is largely a matter of letting go.

Many other writers appear, but these four are my chief influences. If this book should serve as a stepping stone for readers to explore the Rule of St. Benedict, John Cassian, St. John of the Cross, or Blessed Julian of Norwich, I would be most pleased. I should note as well that all the scriptural passages in *Words for Silence* are from the New Revised Standard Version of the Bible.

Finally, none of us makes the journey to God alone. We all need a community to support us in our growth toward awareness and in our practice of ever-deepening surrender and discovery of our true selves in God. My journey has taken place in the context of a monastic community. Without this community of mutual friendship and care, of theological challenge, spiritual balance, and liturgical richness (and good manual labor!), I could never have taken even one step on the contemplative way. Fr. John-Julian Swanson founded the Order of Julian more than twenty-five years ago, inspired by Mother Julian in his vision of a contemplative monastic order that would retrieve the mystical and spiritual teachings of the Christian and especially the Anglican tradition. My debt to him and to all the members of the Order, who have shown me such forgiveness and love, is endless.

My community has also done a great deal of work to make this book possible. My thanks go out to them for the hours of work they have put into the manuscript, as well as to all those who have encouraged me to share these teachings more widely.

Without such urging, I never would have taken on the project. An oblate of the Order of Julian of Norwich, Brenda Weems, provided me with a first critical reading. Patricia Nakamura, an associate of the Order, provided much needed help in editing and shaping the manuscript. Jon Sweeney at Paraclete Press has also been amazingly helpful.

May these words lead you, my reader, into your own silence where you may be still and know that you, without any of the fuss and glamour of life, are already one with God. May these words remind you that you are part of a vast community, a cloud of witnesses, who has journeyed on this path before you and will journey after you. This great tradition is here to teach, console, challenge, and inspire you. May these words be words for the silence where earth and heaven meet, where God is present in creation, where you and everything else are knit together in love.

ADVENT

I N THE MONASTERY, ADVENT is an intensely contemplative time of silence and waiting. The harvesting and freezing of garden crops has ended and with the first snowfall all work on the grounds comes to an end. Shredded leaves steam aromatically in the compost heap and icicles drip as they grow from the chapel gutters through the short days and long nights.

The Advent liturgy, with its vestments of dark purple and blue, is at once penitential and promising. The season begins with John the Baptist, warnings about the end of time, the dissolution of creation, and the nearing Day of Judgment. It ends with the stirring of divine life in the womb of the Blessed Virgin Mary. The festivities of Christmas do not make an entrance until the twenty-fourth day of December, when the monastery and chapel are decorated and the smell of pastries and cookies wafts from the kitchen.

The six meditations in the following section have been chosen for their contemplative tone, their call to interior presence and silence, and their evocation of mystery at the heart of our lives: our waiting upon the Word.

Advent
and the End of Time

THE FIRST WEEK OF ADVENT MARKS THE START of a new liturgical year in Christ. It is a time of darkness, of hidden pregnancy, of waiting. The seed of the kingdom of God, the seed that will germinate at Christmas, sprout in Epiphany, grow through Lent, blossom at Easter, and bear its seven-fold fruit at Pentecost, is sown in the dark soil of Advent. The new life of God is already within us, even though we may see, feel, and understand nothing. Patience and faith are called for.

For the earliest Christians, Advent was an eschatological time, meaning a time when they awaited the end of the world and the Second Coming of Christ. They had a sense that everything was about to pass away: the earth and the heavens consumed by fire. We don't have to believe literally in an immanent second coming in order to enter completely into the spiritual reality of these images, and so into the spiritual heart of Advent as it was understood most anciently.

Julian of Norwich tells us that in every moment of this life the soul experiences itself at the very moment of its being taken by God! This is intense. She means that at some level, usually far under our chattering minds and undulating emotions, the soul is right there with God, and feels itself to be always at the very moment of union with God. This consciousness haunts all of human life, even the most worldly and self-confident. In the inmost depths of our being we are at the very edge, at the final moment before tipping over into union, into ecstasy.

For the contemplative spirit, Advent is thus a time at the very start of the liturgical year to enter into this place where we know ourselves as before God and about to fall into the full Mystery and Life and Beatitude of God. We don't force this or any kind of encounter—our job is rather that of letting everything else go, sitting quietly, attaching to nothing, until this divine truth, this seed of the kingdom in us, can germinate into our conscious awareness.

As Advent is just such a time of quiet attendance and awaiting, we might wish to take up a particular spiritual practice for the season that brings special calm or quiet. We might, for instance, reduce or eliminate our use of entertainment media such as TV, radio, random Web use, or movies. The time gained by such a media-fast can be used to learn how to meditate, or to rejuvenate a silent prayer practice. There are many books on Christian meditation or Centering Prayer, and they are widely available. Alternately, we may decide to spend a few extra minutes every morning keeping a journal, or keeping silence with a scriptural text, listening to its meanings echo through our lives. What would it look like for Christ to be born in our lives? If we have a spiritual friend or director, we might talk about keeping an Advent practice together. If we have a prayer corner in our homes, it can be a powerful symbolic action to remove almost all the books and icons and candles, just keeping one or two items as we wait with new simplicity for our Lord. We might also spend our free time each Advent reading the works of a new mystic or saint—Julian of Norwich, John of the Cross, Thérèse of Lisieux, and Bernard of Clairvaux all come readily to mind. If we are at a loss when it comes to finding such a saint, we can ask a spiritual friend or parish priest for advice. We could also read a book of collected sayings from the saints and mystics until we light on one with whom we feel strong resonance. Saints are important for our journey because they show us new possibilities for our own lives; they stir up our imaginations and open our hearts and minds to what is most real in us. Best of all, Advent is a time to quiet the clamoring anxieties and desires in us, to be silent and to wait as a cup or bowl to be filled with the gift of God's own life.

Going Beneath the Surface of Life

W HEN ONE PERSON IN A FAMILY, in a parish, in a workplace begins to practice being really alive and present in the present moment, not trapped in distractions in her head or lost in his heart, that person is like a burning candle carried into a dark room. People in that person's family or workplace had been sitting in the dark, without even realizing it, thinking that darkness was as bright as things could get. But now, because of the beaming brightness of that person's recollected and whole presence, they are able to see and know deep within themselves just how much more there can be to their religion or their faith. But still, it is only one candle, and the room is still dark. When the flame is passed from person to person until there are many candles burning, then we can really see! Contemplative practice—not just when we are sitting in silent prayer, but the manner in which we live our whole lives—offers a remarkable witness to the possibility of loving God with one's whole heart and soul and mind and strength, with every breath. And when a circle of like-minded friends begins to gather to support each other in the life of contemplative prayer and presence, the witness of each person is strengthened and the community becomes like a circle of lamps on lamp stands, even a great fire of love. This is why so many people find it essential to join or develop local groups for contemplative prayer, or spirituality groups in their parishes.

Such communal support is almost essential, because when we talk about prayer and presence and mindfulness, we are not talking about a technique that can be easily applied to suddenly make life easier. We are talking about the cracking open of a current way of life so that something totally new can be born. This is not merely a matter of sitting in prayer for one or two hours a day—not at all. It is going down under the myriad surface attractions and constant jangling, media-driven alarms of modern life in order to discover something more real, more true to itself. It is a truism that suffering of any kind—sickness, grief, or failure—can drive us under the surface of life. Certainly the deepening and maturing effect of suffering is testified to in the lives of many saints and mystics and ordinary contemplatives.

In Advent, we might do well to recognize the spiritual suffering of God's apparent absence from our lives as itself being a kind of goad to our spiritual maturation. If we talked with our fellow Christians about their inner lives, we might be shocked to learn just how many of us live, day in and day out, with a pervasive sense of divine absence, or at least a longing for a God who seems not fully here, fully with us. Advent can be a season when, instead of trying to cover up this emptiness, we allow ourselves to feel it deeply. We let it ring through us. We have received the promise that in our emptiness a fullness will be born and in that darkness, a light. Just allowing ourselves to be aware of the suffering of not having God as we would like allows God to be born to us in a newer, deeper way. This is how we are progressively deepened, and this is how our presence becomes more settled and more profound, and able to bring light into a darkened room.

⟶ *Giving Everything Away* ⟵

T HROUGHOUT THE HISTORY OF CHRISTIANITY there have been missionaries who have revealed what it means to give everything to God. Abandoning everything familiar and comforting, they put their lives entirely at God's disposal, journeying out into strange lands and bearing the fire of the gospel and of God's Love. We see in their lives a radical commitment to Christ.

A person called to a more consistent and disciplined life of prayer and meditation in the Church is not likely to journey to far-off lands, nor have a dangerous passage through unknown territories, at least in an external sense! We stay where we are and fulfill our vocation according to our current life situation. Yet, although our lives lack external drama and the public sacrifice of the archetypal missionary losing her life for Christ, our journey into contemplative conversion demands a passion every bit as intense as the passion of a missionary and a self-offering every bit as complete. In the life of daily prayer and disciplined, silent self-offering to God, we journey toward a self-gift in which there is nothing of ourselves held back, no remainder at all. This is our destiny; this is where we are headed.

Advent is a time to reclaim our radical passion and commitment. I think that it is natural for our original zeal to cool, to be troubled by temptations, passions, and moods, or to be hampered with useless and distracting thoughts. Instead of a life of self-gift, we become entangled in harried and anxious self-concern. Instead of trusting in God, we seek power and control over worldly realities. Our life then ceases to be a journey into the strange land, the spiritual wilderness where we live close to the Holy Mystery of God. Instead, we become fussy and hyper-sensitive curators of a collection of the familiar and the comforting, and the cliché. God becomes just one item in our collection of favorite things.

In Advent, with its two saints—John the Baptist and the Blessed Virgin—we return to the original prophetic zeal of our desire for God and the great mystery of our soul's pregnancy with God's own life. Returning to that place of original desire and mystery, we clear our inward lives of all that is unessential, strip away the clutter and the thick accretions that prevent the clean flow of the Spirit. We do this not because this world is intrinsically bad, or because of a puritanical instinct for unreal purity, or a morbid delight in cutting against our own desires. Rather, we do this because we have heard again the voice of the Beloved calling us to a life radically given to him in love. In our heart's response we naturally want to have less and less unnecessary stuff in our lives so that we can have more and more space for the Beloved. God is wooing us now out into the wilderness of a truer life so that we can discover the union with him, a union that asks all and gives all, in an exchange of love, as radical an exchange as that lived by any missionary, any martyr, any saint.

⌒ *In Silence, Receive!* ⌒

D O YOU CARE FOR THE LIFE OF CHRIST,
the life of the faithful,
for all those advancing to
contemplative union?
Let your words be few.

As the psalmist says,
Those who delight in their own words
have death for their shepherd.

The more you talk
the less you are heard,
the less weight each word has.

If your words are negative,
murmuring, or bitter,
still less will you be listened to.

And the more you live in your mental world,
a battle made by your thinking
between right and wrong
and you are fighting for the right,
the less you live in reality.

Jesus came to free us
from the worlds and gods
we create for ourselves,
which are always worlds of violence
and idols demanding sacrifice.
By words we try to impose these worlds
on others, we try to get them
to sacrifice their souls
to us.

Do you want to pray for all people everywhere?
For the life of Christ in all?
For the suffering, beaten down,
lost and despairing?
For peace?
For your own need for union?
Only pray the Our Father.

The New Light is rising!
It is being born in our midst.
In your stillness receive the full
wind-wide giving of that Light.
In your stillness receive
the deep utterance of this word.

Unceasing Prayer

I N THE FIFTH CHAPTER OF FIRST THESSALONIANS, St. Paul writes, "Rejoice always; pray without ceasing; give thanks in all circumstances; for this is the will of God in Christ Jesus for you." In this short passage we discover the whole reality of the life of prayer.

"Always be joyful" reminds me immediately of Blessed Julian of Norwich, who speaks from the heart of the English mystical tradition when she says that the universe is imbued with God's joy, and that we can do nothing more pleasing to God than to release ourselves to this flow of divine gladness. Such joy in God is not mere happiness or feeling good, or a pious emotion we whip up together, but it is the ability to be totally present where we are, whole in ourselves and open in affirmation to the reality around us. As such, it is the end-product of a lifetime of self-surrender.

"Pray continually." These two words are the foundation of the Christian mystical and monastic tradition and add to the admonition to "always be joyful" the sense that such joy, for Christians, is lived out in a relationship of continual, responsive awareness of God. This was sought in every great mystical and monastic revival down through history. The Desert Fathers and Mothers went into the deserts of Egypt and Syria and committed their lives to learn unceasing prayer. The early Benedictines, the Carthusians, and other eremitical renewals all made this the aim of the spiritual life. The idea of becoming a person who prays without ceasing inspired the Cistercian Reform in the twelfth century, the great Carmelite reform of the sixteenth, and the Trappist reform after it. Brother Lawrence and Jean Pierre de Caussade are the most eloquent early modern exponents of this desire. In our own day we see the Centering Prayer movement and John Main's Christian Meditation, which, when practiced correctly, aim also at unceasing prayer.

Finally: "Give thanks for whatever happens." Giving thanks is the original meaning of the word for Eucharist, where we offer thanks to God. Giving thanks for whatever happens can be a kind of Eucharistic offering, where we take the events of the day, and in offering them to God, receive them back as the secret carriers of God's will. Each moment it is at least possible to be an ambassador of God, if only we are brave enough to receive it so.

Of course it is possible to get frustrated when we find ourselves doing the exact opposite of this spiritual counsel from St. Paul. When we begin the spiritual life, and all the way along the journey, we are likely to find ourselves more despairing than joyful, not living in a mode of ceaseless response to God but curled up in self-centeredness, not giving thanks but remaining resentful about what is happening. As we experience the difficulty of becoming people of authentic joy, prayer, and gratitude, we can come to believe that St. Paul, in writing this one line, was waxing romantic and getting too idealistic for his own good. We can think the same of all the great spiritual traditions that have sprung from this one root. So we are tempted to return to semi-Christian lives of half-conversion, the lives of "quiet desperation" that Thoreau saw so many people living.

But what if there is another way of understanding these admonitions? What if St. Paul was not exaggerating or even telling us to achieve some spiritual ideal, but was basically sharing with us something he had experienced for himself: that God's life is a flow of joy, communion, and thanksgiving, and that it is possible for us as human creatures to release ourselves to this flow?

In a similar passage from Philippians, Paul actually gives us practical advice about how to begin our own greater openness to a more intimate life with God. He writes: "The Lord is near. Do not worry about anything, but in everything by prayer and supplication with thanksgiving let your requests be made known to God. And the peace of God, which surpasses all understanding, will guard your hearts and your minds in Christ Jesus." What we see here is not simplistic piety, but hard-won inner clarity in which we are aware of our fears and anxieties and we learn how to offer them to God. We interrupt our anxiety, fears, and resentments as we become conscious of them, and we offer them to God in prayer as they arise, one after another.

This practical measure can begin to transform our desperate lives of unceasing anxiety into the lives of unceasing prayer and peace. We don't grit our teeth and clench our fists and try to be joyful and grateful. Rather, we make it a practice to notice our worries, to interrupt their monologue, and to offer them to God in prayer. That's all. And yet it actually leads, over time, to a participation in God's life as Paul experienced it. It leads to a simplicity that is a joyful offering of self, a transparency to God. It leads to unceasing prayer and communion.

As we walk through Advent, and "the Lord is near," as Paul says, we can ask ourselves what habits of mind, body, emotion, or spirit prevent us from receiving the offering of God's life to us. Why do we sometimes prefer to remain locked into cramped lives of anxiety, ingratitude, fear, and conflict? Why don't we let these things go? Where do we habitually fall into these forms of negativity and why do we fear offering them to God for healing? If we always have the divine life of rejoicing, communion, and peace flowing through us, and if Jesus is the offering of this life into our midst, what habitual sins prevent us from opening ourselves to receive the divine gift?

Hidden
in Ordinary Life

A s ADVENT NEARS ITS END and the Feast of Christ's Nativity draws close, we are in the small hours of the night, the last moments of darkness before the great Light rises with "healing for all humankind in its wings." In our stillness we are aware of salvation history balanced on this one moment in the darkness, poised and waiting for the birth cry of this new Child. We feel ourselves to be like Mary, and our souls to be like that stable in Bethlehem. Everything is still and ready. There is nothing more we can do to prepare, let alone initiate. We wait for the sheer gift of this New Life.

At times such as these—times of silence, of deep trust, and waiting—we can glimpse the remarkable beauty of a life given primarily to intimacy with God in prayer. There are so many wonderful vocations in the Church, vocations that have a high profile, that attract attention and praise, that have some glamour to them. There are vocations of great busyness and decisions and committees, and awesome self-giving is required to live into these faithfully. But if we have followed God deeply into the contemplative way, and understand that an act of deep love and adoration is our primary calling in the Church, it is likely that no one will ever notice! It will not get written up in the parish bulletin. It will not appear in the newspapers.

People called to loving intimacy with God are not usually extraordinary in their outward demeanor. To the movers and shakers of the world, they may seem "ho-hum," with nothing to excite interest or charm. Such people are not only hidden from the flash and glamour of the world, but are often quite homely—in the Middle English sense of the word: "simple, domestic, friendly, straightforward, accessible."

When we find ourselves called in this way of extraordinary love hidden within an ordinary life, we come to understand that our call to divine union is neither deepened nor consummated in earthshaking events or revelations or dramatic happenings. Rather, it is in the homely events of the everyday that our love for God—that deep flow of unceasing desire and praise and celebration—is purified, perfected, and consummated.

Look, for instance, at the many small slights, disappointments, hurts, and annoyances that come to all of us in daily life. For most people these are simply things to be minimized, endured, and forgotten. For the contemplative soul the very pain these pinpricks cause alerts us to places where our anxious self-concern and vanity still remain. We can then offer up ourselves and the small pains to God in the unseen solitude of our hearts. This is also how love is perfected, and finally how love is consummated—often completely hidden, unsung, and unknown to the outside world, in the homely events of everyday life. The vocation to lived intimacy with God proceeds by great strides when we realize this; we stop thinking that it is about spectacular experiences, esoteric meditation techniques, or profound insights and begin living ordinary life as the means of our surrender to and union with God.

The mystery of the incarnation for which we are preparing is the mystery of the divine life being born in what is most lowly and humble. The divine life of love, the life of Christ himself, can be born and made incarnate in the humblest stable: in our lives and our hearts. As people called to interior intimacy with God, we know from experience that the consummation of divine love can happen where no one sees it, or even wants to see it—in the little, unsung moments of everyday life.

CHRISTMAS

CHRISTMAS IS A SHORT, MAGICAL SEASON of feasting and celebrating in the monastery, beginning on Christmas Eve, when we enjoy eggnog and sweets around the Christmas tree while opening gifts sent to the community. The chapel is decorated with poinsettias and garlands and wreathes woven with gold and white ribbons, and the refectory and common rooms are likewise festooned. The Christmas tree, dazzling with its strings of white lights, is covered with ornaments that trace the Order's history, some made by members of the community, going back to the first days of our communal life.

Underneath our enjoyment of the rich food, decorations, and Christmas carols, there is a deeper awareness of just what all this feasting is for: the welcoming of God born to us as a human being in Jesus of Nazareth. Undistracted by mandatory shopping or party-going, we are able to open our imaginations to the stories of Jesus' birth. Receiving these stories and images into ourselves and holding them with love in our imaginations, we allow God to speak deeply to us through them. Such divine speaking in the silent hours of our prayer not only opens our hearts and minds, but has creative power to change who we are, to conform us more to Jesus as God made flesh.

The handful of meditations in this section focus on the wonder of God's Incarnation of the Son of God, this tremendous sign of the goodness of creation and God's choice for loving union with us.

Wandering with
Holy Women and the Wise Men

IN THE MONASTERY WHERE I LIVE it is a Christmas tradition that the figurines of the Magi and the camels spend twelve days wandering from the Christmas tree all around the monastery, hopefully to arrive, twelve days later, at the crèche on the vigil of the Epiphany. The novice brothers and sisters move them about secretly so that the Magi and camels surprise you as they appear progressively in stairwells, windowsills, bookshelves, and even on top of the fax machine. One year a sister even made the Magi a tiny map of ancient Palestine.

This intra-monastic journey-in-miniature, with its humor and playfulness, has always been for me a symbol of our journey to Christ, a journey that is never straight or direct, but circuitous, ambiguous, wandering, going, as it appears to us, backward and forward. Two things have struck me most about this journey.

The first is that this journey, in this life, has no end. It will stretch until our very last breath, and perhaps even beyond that. The only contentment we can have is not the contentment of final arrival, but the contentment of people who have made a definitive and all-encompassing choice to follow the deepest calling of their hearts. The great St. Teresa of Avila suffered for years from living in an in-between state, being at once sort-of-religious in her convent and still sort-of-worldly, having one foot in both worlds. She had no inner contentment because she refused to set out, once for all and with total commitment, on the journey. St. Teresa only discovered some measure of inner peace when she gave herself over completely to God and God's desire for her.

Contentment is found in choosing the journey to God as the main reality of our lives, fully aware as we choose it that this journey will likely keep on going for the whole of our lives. We make a measured, sober, and loving choice for the long haul. And we have to equip ourselves properly for the lifelong backward and forward journey that we find ourselves on. We need a measure of modesty, humility, and joy in small things, balance, and a realistic and wise sense of what our spiritual practice will be, if we are to walk this path in a way that brings life and joy to ourselves and those closest to us.

The second thing that strikes me about this lifelong journey to Christ is that in many ways it is a calling to journey out of the familiar, or, more accurately, to suffer a radical dislocation of ourselves out of the familiar. Reading about the lives of people who have been taken by God, like St. Teresa of Avila or her companion, St. John of the Cross, we always find evidence of profound dislocation, something that jarred them loose from the status quo and forced them to search for a deeper commitment, often with considerable suffering. Their lives had to be broken open, so that God could pour in his grace. Like Abraham who was asked by God to leave his home, like the Magi wandering from the East toward Jerusalem, like Teresa of Avila with her illnesses and unquiet emotional life, we begin our journey by suffering a dislocation at God's hands.

In the monastic tradition, there is indeed a love of customary practices, love of the physical place of the monastery and its ground, and a love of patterned, rhythmic, cyclical life. Outside the monastery, most everyone will need to put down roots in a particular place with particular customs and habits. I am not saying here that these things have to be disturbed intentionally, as such rootedness and customs help to quiet the spirit and open it to God. Rather, I am talking about the inner experience of dislocation, happening in the midst of the ordinary, customary, and habitual. Indeed, everyone walking the spiritual and contemplative way will have a need precisely for these socially held, supportive outward structures. Even simple, understood customs like waking up in the morning at about the same time and getting ready for the day mindfully and peacefully, perhaps with time for silence and prayer, can have a huge grounding and centering effect. Then, when God does come—when God jars our inner life loose, when God asks us to confront some inner pain or loss and to journey to divine intimacy—we will be ready and able to do so.

⤳ The Nameless Child ⤶

I N THE WEEK BETWEEN CHRISTMAS and the Feast of the Holy Name, the Christ-child, born of Mary, is still without a name. We do not have a name for this presence of God among us; we don't know what to call it. Unlimited by any preconceived notions, the child is here with us simply and totally. Real faith and hope are activated when we consciously choose to give this child space and time within the boundaries of our personal existence—within our imaginations, hearts, minds, and memories. We give the divine word, uttered into human flesh, this incomparable and incomprehensible gift, room and place within ourselves where it can be, where it can live, where it can speak. Practically this means setting aside time each day, no matter how little, to meditate and ruminate on Scripture, or to pray the Rosary, or to look with open simplicity at the image presented by an icon. God's Word, Jesus, becomes important enough to us that we take the time and make the space to let him enter us and speak as he wills within us.

When the contemplative life is first born in us, when we feel ourselves called to special intimacy with the God whom we have allowed into ourselves in our quiet rumination on the Word made flesh, we might not even have a name for what is happening, nor an understanding of what it means, or where it is going. Instead, we experience an unsettling awareness that something new and unknown, yet something that lays claim to the whole meaning and passion of our life, has been born in the center of our souls out of the divine word and image that we have held there by love in our daily prayers and devotions. We sense that within us there is a new presence, cloaked in mystery. We do not know how our lives will flow with this mystery now born within us. We don't yet even have a name for this newborn divine life, we don't know what it will look like as it matures.

And yet, for all this unknowability, the basic need for each contemplative beginner is clear. As we become aware of this unsettling presence of God in us, each of us has to find practical, everyday ways to open ourselves to its urgency, to attend to its new life, and to learn from it how to live anew. Once again this means taking time for God, but also learning, in the midst of life, how to turn inward. Even as we are busy in outward affairs, we learn how to make small, interior acts of love and surrender. We offer up our pains, we share with God our joys, we ask God to come and live within us. We return again and again in the course of a day to a spiritual insight or an inspiration drawn from our morning devotions. We repeat within ourselves a favorite verse of Scripture or a devotional phrase in order to recall ourselves to our true reality. This we can do even as we take care of ordinary tasks and responsibilities.

If we live this way, we can then greet every day as another in which we are under the special tutelage of this Nameless New Life in our midst. Each day is a day in the divine school of the Nameless One who wishes to lead us further into himself. Our job is to love, to make space and time in our lives for this One who has come into our lives, and to return to him repeatedly through the day, learning to abide in him. If we do this, then the life of intimacy with God, born into our midst, will unfold and extend its energies into the whole of our existence.

We will be moved and ordered according to the inescapable, ineluctable, non-deducible wisdom of Love who is ordering all things sweetly in our midst—ordering all things around this nameless Child.

No Leaning, No Slouching

THE WORD BECAME FLESH AND DWELT AMONG US.

The eternal Word of God lived a human life in Jesus. God was fully present in time. This is the core of what theologians call the incarnational principle, in which every atom of creation, every moment of time, is understood as possibly filled with the fullness of God's eternal reality and life. The fullness of God's Self was present in Jesus, and as a result of God's indwelling Spirit, we can begin to live the moments of our lives as likewise filled with God, open to the full reality of the eternal Word. This new potential of creation to bear the fullness of God's life and light is what we celebrate at Christmas. It is what Jesus' birth announces.

Lest this seem too exalted, so theological that it can't really help us in everyday life, I suggest that we can actually experience and learn to live this reality. We don't have to think a great deal about it (thinking in this way will likely prove unhelpful), nor do we push ourselves to feel pious emotions or to live at an impossibly high pitch of spiritual intensity. Such efforts usually end in a collapse into despair, and betray a prominent amount of self-centered desire.

Throughout this book I will be touching again and again on the art of surrender, the process of letting go to God, which as an action of release and openness is the core of the Christian and contemplative way. It is the basic reality of living in intimacy with God in which our small temporal lives flow out into an eternal reality just as Jesus' life did. For now, I would like to introduce one very helpful, concise practice that, if taken into ordinary life, will reveal when we have given way to self-centeredness and provides a powerful bodily metaphor for the experience of self-surrender. I call it "no leaning, no slouching."

Human beings are not primarily thoughts nor emotions. We are bodies, living in space and time. Our physical posture, how we are holding our bodies, is a direct indicator of what is happening in our spirit.

When we lean forward, our spirits are, as it were, lunging out of the present moment, eager to grasp the future. Another way of saying this is that we have become anxious and greedy. We are living in a spirit of anxious self-concern to get what we want. The present moment is gone, thus our eternal reality in God is gone. All that we are left with is the drama of our anxious selves lunging forward in time to get what we desire.

By *no leaning*, I mean that our bodily stance is perfectly upright, which indicates presence, awareness, and selflessness. We are present in this moment to what is. We are here and now.

Slouching, like leaning, is also a way of denying the sacrament of the Now and refusing the present moment. Instead of leaning through the present toward something else in the future, we slouch—we curl into ourselves and withdraw from reality, both present and future. This is especially tempting when we are sad or tired. We slouch out of the present moment, away from the future. We cease to be here, upright, where communion is possible. Slouching is a refusal of the moment, a refusal of others, of our life situation. We want to get away from it all.

Can we live without leaning and without slouching? Can we live all of the time in uprightness, in presence, sharp and attentive? I believe we can. What it requires is practice. We can practice neither leaning nor slouching when we are listening to others, when we are walking or on errands, or when we are at our desks.

My community knows from experience that if I make the effort to sit upright during a communal conversation, if I suddenly lift my head, sit aligned on my spine, and place my hands mindfully in my lap, I am making an effort to be fully present to what is being said and fully present to God's Spirit in the meeting. I am opening myself up like a perfectly still, tuned-in antenna for God in that moment. Neither leaning forward in anxiety to make sure my point is heard, nor withdrawing from the conversation by sullenly slouching into my chair, I am listening for the eternal Word of God incarnate in us in that moment of time. I feel intensely alive when I do this, because I am intensely present, and lifted clear out of my anxious and depressive feelings.

If you have read one or two books on meditation or contemplative prayer, you will have noted that it is universally advised to neither lean nor slouch in meditation, but to sit upright. This is taught in almost every meditative practice. Simply by adjusting our posture we adjust our spirits, we align ourselves with the eternal Now that just *is* this moment in time. And just as we are advised to spend a half hour in physical exercise each day so that the rest of our lives is lived from a place of bodily health, so we are advised in every contemplative, spiritual tradition to set apart some time each day to practice neither leaning nor slouching, but in contemplative stillness, sitting upright and present to what is.

⟶ EPIPHANY

E PIPHANY IS ONE OF OUR LEAST-CELEBRATED SEASONS. It runs from the feast of the Epiphany on January 6 to Ash Wednesday (a moveable day) and thus can be as little as four or as many as eight weeks long.

But the fact of Epiphany being less-celebrated than Christmas or Easter does not mean it is spiritually or theologically negligible, a blank time between the feasting of Christmas and the fasting of Lent. The name *Epiphany* comes from the Greek verb meaning *to reveal,* and contains a wonderful breadth of meaning including the experience of insight, the showing forth of divine glory, and the specifically Christian sense of Jesus' being revealed as the Christ to the non-Jewish peoples.

The season of Epiphany thus resounds with two enormous theological themes: God's offering of a loving covenant to all the peoples of the world and the Divine Glory being revealed in Jesus, the Light from Light, as we say in the Nicene Creed, with ever-increasing authority and power. The Last Sunday of Epiphany focuses on the Gospel account of the transfiguration of Jesus by divine light as he turns to face his death and ultimate triumph in Jerusalem.

The meditations in this short section touch on these themes of light and illumination, as well as the meaning of the contemplative vocation. Those called to lives of interior prayer, and surrendering to God in the present moment, are not freed from the great commission to take Christ to all peoples. However, the mode of our missionary endeavor is different; it will be most powerfully offered through the manner and quality of our presence. The understanding of what it means to live with Christ and bring others to life in him takes on a simplicity and depth. It has less to do with verbal protestations and more with an evolving awareness of the divine presence everywhere.

Glory Without the Sword

I N THE ANCIENT WORLD, *doxa*, translated as glory, referred originally to the athlete who had just won a great victory. Even in our day we are familiar with this experience of "pagan" glory: a baseball star radiates *doxa* after he has hit the game-winning home run. The athlete becomes for a moment more than human, elevated above us as an object of fascination and adulation, and we can't wait to hear news about this greatness in our midst. We gravitate toward and circle around the phenomenon of pagan glory, wherever it appears, like moths around a candle flame.

During the season of Epiphany, the Church asks us to pray that "illumined by your Word and Sacraments, we may shine with the radiance of Christ's glory that He may be known, worshiped, and obeyed to the ends of the earth." It is an awesome thing to pray that we ourselves may shine with the radiance of Christ's own glory, but it begs the question of just what Christ's glory is, and how this is realized in our lives.

Many hymns attempt to make Christ glorious along the pagan lines of the great athlete or warrior who wins our salvation. But there is always a problem with these metaphors, because pagan glory is always won in competition or combat over against others. For one person to be glorious in this way, other people have to be defeated or destroyed. For one to be the winner there has to be a multitude of losers. Pagan glory is essentially agonistic, conflictual, tinged with the blood of the conquered and based in violence.

Christ's glory is not the pagan glory of one ego exalted to superhuman status over the vanquished bodies of the losers. The stunning revelation at the heart of the gospel is that Jesus walked the way of the ultimate loser, apparently failing in his mission, then betrayed by his disciples, then tortured and killed on the dung heap outside Jerusalem. Yes, Christ is in fact raised from the dead and so raised to glory, to doxa, but look at how different this glory is: when the resurrected Christ walks into the room where his disciples are hiding, trying to save their own skins and thus perpetuating their betrayal of him, Jesus not only bids them peace, but empowers them to go and take his love and his truth to others. Jesus' glory is not based in having won anything on the battlefield of history. It is not based in competition. Jesus' glory, which he offers to share with us, is rather the eternal, pacific flow of bliss and union with all things, in humility and joy. This is the eternal glory, the life of joyful radiance and loving connectedness that God is. The Old Testament description of Wisdom captures this well:

There is in [Wisdom] a spirit that is intelligent, holy,
unique, manifold, subtle,
mobile, clear, unpolluted,
distinct, invulnerable, loving the good, keen,
irresistible, beneficent, humane,
steadfast, sure, free from anxiety,
all-powerful, overseeing all,
and penetrating through all spirits
that are intelligent, pure, and altogether subtle.
For wisdom is more mobile than any motion;

because of her pureness she pervades and penetrates all things.
For she is a breath of the power of God
and a pure emanation of the glory of the Almighty;
therefore nothing defiled gains entrance into her. . . .
Although she is but one, she can do all things
and while remaining in herself, she renews all things.
(Wisdom 7:22–27a)

Christ has this kind of glory. He has no competitors, and he vanquishes no one. He traveled more painfully into loss than any of us can imagine, giving everything away, and in loving obedience to God remained utterly transparent and so perfectly revelatory of the presence and will of God. The eternal benediction of divine light and glory, bliss and joy, flows through him without any effort, pervading and renewing all things.

Through our lives of contemplative practice and prayer, we ourselves are brought to experience a depth of being not constituted by conflict. Illumined by God's mysterious self-communication in our depths, we begin, perhaps unconsciously, to allow the glorious life of God, where there is no wrath or contradiction, to flow through us. There is no struggle, no fuss, no bother. This is the reality of out-flowing love establishing and moving through us in peace, simplicity, and gift. Contemplative prayer and the practice of living deeply in the present moment slowly slake our need for ego-glory through conflict against others or against reality itself, and allow us to receive the clear, peaceful, self-bestowal of God. We come to shine more with the radiance of Christ's own glory and we become missionaries of a new way of being—Christ's way of being in loving surrender and generative peace.

The Lord and the Savior

S EVERAL YEARS AGO WHEN OUR CHAPEL was being built, I
had a conversation with an evangelical Christian who was
working in our future sacristy. Knowing that he was building
a chapel for us, he asked what Jesus meant to me. I said, "He
means everything!" And in my zeal I listed a number of the great
Christological titles, from the Alpha all the way down to the
Omega. Yet no matter what I said, he still looked disappointed
and finally he just shrugged and went his way. A sister who had
spent a good deal of her life in Texas later informed me that I
had missed the one and only phrase he was listening for, that
Jesus was my Lord and Savior, a verbal formula as critical to
some evangelicals as the papacy is to some Roman Catholics.

In one of our collects for the season of Epiphany, we ask
God to grant "that all who are baptized into [Jesus'] Name may
keep the covenant they have made, and boldly confess him as
Lord and Savior." There it is: Lord and Savior. But in order
for this phrase to be more to us than a magical incantation or
a secret handshake, we have to do the hard work of translating
its meaning into speech that even non-Christians could understand, or that at least meets their concerns halfway.

The Church has always done this with the Faith. For the
early church fathers, Neoplatonism and stoicism were just such
a language. In the medieval era, St. Thomas Aquinas used a
combination of Neoplatonic mysticism with hardheaded,
scientific Aristotelianism to achieve a marvelous theological
synthesis. For the Oxford movement in nineteenth-century

Anglicanism, the Romantic rebellion against the Enlightenment and a cultural, neo-Gothic enthusiasm gave them a vehicle to retrieve and re-present the mystical depths of Christianity. Every language we choose will limit the witness at the same time as it makes it possible. But it is no good to simply repeat a formula, "Jesus is Lord and Savior," until other people, for reasons of emotional or social coercion, jump on board and start repeating the phrase themselves.

For Christians on the contemplative way, we have a dual witness. To our fellow-Christians we are called to share our experience of increasing intimacy with God in silence and practiced surrender, and invite them into this deep way of knowing and loving and responding to our Lord. To our fellow contemplatives who are not a part of the Church, who have perhaps renounced the Church because it seemed to them superficial or misguided, who define themselves as spiritual but not religious, we can share the significance of Christian faith in our practice of contemplative spirituality. Our common contemplative experience of prayer, meditation, and mindfulness gives us a vehicle to do this.

Ours is a spirituality of surrender, of letting go, and of discovering a whole new mode of life within that surrender. The Christian language for this is death and resurrection. We journey deeper and deeper into letting go of ourselves until there seems to be almost nothing left, yet find ourselves simultaneously alive with a new vibrancy that transcends our old life completely. Jesus is our Lord because he showed us what it means to live and die in this way. And he demanded clearly of his disciples: "Anyone who wants to be a follower of mine must renounce self . . . he who loses his life for my sake and for the gospel will find it." Jesus is also our Savior because we experience him as giving us his own life of immediacy and union with the Father, a life characterized by presence, compassion, and transparent awareness, values that are central to spiritual but not religious contemplatives.

If I were to encounter my evangelical friend again, I would say clearly to him that Jesus is my Lord and Savior. But I would also go on to share with him how deep my experience has been of Jesus in silent prayer, and in the practice of mindfulness in everyday life. I would tell him that the only place where I can really be a Christian, can really know Jesus as the Lord who leads me to resurrected life and the Savior who gives me that life freely and spontaneously, is in the present moment.

The Art of Surrender

E VERY NIGHT IN THE MONASTERY WE END our half hour of communal silent prayer with a prayer taken from Julian of Norwich's *Revelations of Divine Love*: "God, of Thy goodness, give me Thyself; for Thou art enough to me, and I can ask nothing that is less that can be full honor to Thee. And if I ask anything that is less, ever shall I be in want, for only in Thee have I all" (*Lesson*, Chapter 5).[1]

We ask God in this prayer not to give us what is agreeable or even what we think is right and good, but to give us only God in the mystery of Godself. We pray for God's presence because we recognize that anything less than God will never be enough for us.

This is a radical way of understanding ourselves—to believe that we will never be satisfied with any created reality, with anything we could find or experience in creation, anything we possess or think or know or feel. This extends even to our experiences of God considered as things we can have or attain. No experience, no matter how exalted, is enough to bring us to rest. But if even the mostly exalted spiritual experience won't satisfy us, what will? Don't we hope that in the end some vast experience of God will finally satisfy us?

There is only one thing that ever brings us to rest or satisfaction—the unconditioned surrender of ourselves to God. As the mystics tell us, when we are able to make this offering of ourselves, the life of God suddenly breaks through. The act of surrender and the gift of God's satisfying fullness are in fact two sides of the same coin. The contemplative is one who practices this habitually.

But how do we surrender to God? What does it mean to practice surrender? How does this become a way of life? Practicing surrender, which is the same as living in intimacy with God, or the contemplative way, does not mean becoming passive or indifferent to reality or having no eager initiative in life. Still less does it mean tolerating injustice or abuse. Rather, practicing surrender means accepting the whole reality of this present moment as the *starting point* for the rest of my life, a continually renewed starting point. Usually this means walking through three steps:

1. We become consciously aware of resistance in ourselves to the present reality we are in. This is the opposite of surrender. We are fighting against and refusing reality. We learn to feel this in our bodies. Our breathing becomes rapid, our chest and shoulders tighten, our stomach hurts, our forehead contracts. Such inner resistance to the reality we are in has no beneficial or creative power. It is more akin to denial. It is an inward attitude of pushing away the present moment or life situation, a refusal to accept it as real.

2. Looking deeply into this refusal, we might find beneath it a great pain or fear. There are reasons why we have unconsciously risen up into a refusal of what is right before us, a refusal to accept it and deal with it.

3. As we become aware of the underlying pain that drives our refusal and as we see how this refusal only perpetuates the suffering and paralyzes our initiative, an act of surrender arises in us. I don't say we grit our teeth and surrender, but that the surrender that Jesus himself lived and modeled for us in Gethsemane rises up in us. When this happens, we experience ourselves letting go of the refusal, allowing our suffering to flow completely through and out of us, and we turn ourselves around from denial into a full acceptance of this moment, this life situation as the only place where God is actually present in our lives, the only place that is real. A life situation we couldn't even bear to face before becomes, in this moment, the context for God's loving initiative and action and empowerment in our lives.

Practicing surrender as a movement from paralyzing refusal to acceptance and action is something Christ invites us to in the largest, most all-encompassing life tragedies such as the loss of a loved one or a failed relationship. But it is helpful to begin with smaller, trivial refusals: with our anger at a line at the grocery store being so long, or with a sad mood at the start of a challenging day. Instead of just sailing along in our anger or drifting down under a fog of sadness, we can become aware of how we are feeling these refusals in our body. And, if these are relatively superficial refusals, we might be able to practice immediately letting go of them and turning ourselves around to face fully into this present moment or situation as God's will for the starting point of our lives. Instead of just hating the present moment and waiting for a better one to come along, we find ourselves, in our acceptance of it, empowered to make a choice about it. We can always leave the queue. We can make choices to moderate the difficulty of a day ahead. Then we are no longer experiencing ourselves as helpless victims in lives out of our control, but as courageous, strong people, who are choosing to negotiate life's challenges in a mindful, conscious, committed way, as part of our commitment to serve and love God in all things. Working with such small, everyday experiences builds up our habit of surrender until we perhaps are able to look at the more difficult and extensive issues in our lives.

Living in intimacy with God is nothing less or more than building up a strong inner habit (1) of awareness, (2) of letting go of refusal, and (3) of conscious choice and initiative in a desire to serve God. As we explore living this way, what we discover is the possibility of life as communion with God, life just as Jesus lived. God's giving us the fullness of Godself is not found in having exalted thoughts or feelings about God or even praying to God a lot. God's giving us Godself in contemplative union is not found in discrete spiritual experiences, no matter how special or refined. It is found rather in a life lived in surrender and conscious action, in which we experience ourselves as living one life with God—surrendering all refusal, receiving the energy of God, and flowing out with this into conscious, selfless action. This is the only satisfying reality there is.

God, of your goodness, give me yourself and in doing so give me my true self. If I ask for anything that is less, I will still be in want, for only in you have I all that I need.

Presence Workers

I N OUR WORLD TODAY WE NEED NOTHING more urgently than
people engaged in transformative protest and action from
a heart transformed by contemplation. This sounds exalted,
beyond the reach of ordinary people, but it becomes less so if
we understand the process that gets us there.

Most of us begin the Christian life from an active standpoint:
we want to do or think or experience things that somehow make
a difference in ourselves, in others, or in the world. We find
ourselves called into a plethora of ministries and committees
and action groups.

If we persevere with this and with prayer, we will after a while
begin to experience a different calling, an inner urgency. We
become aware of God wanting us just for ourselves, regardless
of what we initiate or achieve. We begin to understand what
John of the Cross meant when he said that one act of authentic
love for God is worth more than a lifetime of action. Such acts
of authentic love for God are our initiation into the inner life
of Jesus, into the sacred heart that beats at the center of the
cosmos, giving life and love and light to all.

Thus begins the contemplative journey, described as a process
of learning how to live close to God, habitually in touch with
God, intimate with and responsive to God's every desire.
We begin to realize that much of our previous activity and
prayer flowed from anxiety and grasping, self-centered desire.
We were acting either out of fear or a drive to get something
for ourselves. Even if the sought-after end of our prayer or

action was something laudable, we see that it is stained by the fundamental selfishness. It sounds harsh, but we see that we were basically acting and using God for ourselves. This is what St. Bernard of Clairvaux, the eleventh-century mystic and monk, called "loving God for our own sake." Passing through the pain of this shocking knowledge, we become more sensitive and careful in our listening for God's will and more surrendered in our response to him. We begin to understand that our union with God happens in a process of continual letting go, continual surrender, yielding the gates of our heart to him continually. Our life shifts at this point. We take up meditative practices and silent prayer in order to practice our surrender. Going on retreats, as an act of letting go of our life-projects altogether in order to be wholly present to God, becomes more important and life giving. We begin to love God for God's sake, learning how to give ourselves away to him. Vast healing and the transformation of ourselves in love can happen as we learn how to walk in this contemplative mode.

But after a while of this, we enter another stage. This is where divine love for the world, for the rest of humanity, becomes a burning urgency in us, and we are carried on the tide of this divine love back into the world to initiate action that brings healing and hope to our brothers and sisters. When we reach this point, we are beginning to live the full life of Jesus, retiring at times into intense moments of union and surrender to the Father and flowing out at other times into the world in love.

In the monastery, this happens over a period of many years and is part of the ordinary formation process. When persons first enter the community, they have a thousand tasks to learn, a whole new tradition and values to absorb, and practices to engage. They have the task of working alongside God to build themselves up as good, committed, solid monks and nuns. Given the pattern of our life—praying in chapel five times a day, retiring into silent prayer for an hour a day, going on regular retreats—this naturally leads monastics to a place where they become aware of God's desire for the purification of the motives behind their lives. They see that all their action in the community has been about themselves, driven by underlying anxiety, and is basically self-centered. They begin to experience and know the centrality of surrender, and letting go, and the newfound intimacy with God that is nothing less than life-changing. The inner pain that was unconsciously driving their self-centered action is directly opened to divine love, often with great suffering. They are in a process of learning divine intimacy in yielding and suffering, comforted by a sense that they are, in a hidden way, getting in touch with a whole new depth of existence and a tremendous power and wholeness within themselves. This usually happens in the middle years of the monastic journey. Finally, at the end of the process, these brothers and sisters, healed in themselves and strong in habits of inner surrender, are re-inspired to action and service for God's sake. Their work, their programs, their initiatives in the community and beyond flow now not from anxiety or selfishness, but from the surging of divine love through them. Often this means they will assume leadership and pastoral responsibilities in the community.

All of us, whether in a monastery or not, who reach this stage on the spiritual journey are what I call "presence workers." We know firsthand that our most important gift to the world is in fact the quality of presence, which is to say the quality of love, that we bring to each moment of the day, each encounter, each action. We are carried along in the divine presence and we carry it with us. We have learned how to live, through *years* of practice, in surrendered intimacy with God. But this very intimacy and surrender now carries us out into creative and transformative action in the world, action that has at its center a vast simplicity, an utter transparency to God's life and love. Whether in contemplative stillness or heroic action, we are witnessing to God's presence and life. It is all one love.

In a sense, there is nothing one can do to hasten oneself along in this journey. An eagerness to get somewhere, to achieve something, no matter how spiritual, is in fact a clear sign that we are still walking in the path of unreformed action, trying to get something for ourselves. What we can bring however is a new awareness that something more is possible for our lives, and to take up practices that carry us into a kind of sustained vulnerability to God as he calls us into contemplative intimacy, a new life of surrender, and then out into transformed and transparent action.

Those of us who seek to do God's will and desire to yield ourselves to the process that leads to transformed and transforming action can do nothing more helpful than commit ourselves to a rule of life under spiritual direction, within the framework of a worshiping community. Until we engage a regular rule of life, and until we are willing to see ordinary life as the place of our encounter with God, exactly as it is, we will be unable to grow spiritually. Our lives will remain firmly centered on ourselves, our fears, anxieties, and desires. But once we commit to a spiritual rule of life, then we begin to walk in the way that leads toward intimacy and presence and action. We become presence workers in the world, an Epiphany of God's presence, and Jesus' life and energy here and now.

It Is Good That We Are Here

I N THE STORY OF THE TRANSFIGURATION, Jesus takes Peter, James, and John up a mountain to pray. As Jesus prays, he is transformed, with his clothes becoming "dazzling white." Moses, the lawgiver, and Elijah, the prophet, come to speak to Jesus about the mission he is to fulfill in Jerusalem. At this point, Peter wakes up with the others and says, "Lord, it is good that we are here."

"It is good that we are here." In the Gospel, this line is part of Peter's misunderstanding. He is so overwhelmed by what he is seeing that he wants to remain there permanently. He wants to build booths in which they could stay.

There are moments in each of our lives when the ordinary flesh and bones of life are transfigured, when our consciousness stands in "raiment white and glistening" before the mystery of Being Itself. For that brief moment, we may know, with St. Peter, how deeply, amazingly, shockingly good it is that we are all here.

I experienced this first in my life before coming to the monastery, when I first fell in love. It was an amazing gift that combined adoration and celebration, almost blinding in its intensity, the most painful joyfulness of being completely present and alive. But there are other moments, less tumultuous now and more mature: sitting in my cell and listening to the rain fall. Or watching the morning light rise over the world in a sheer magnificence of peace and warmth and offering. Or holding the host at Mass, knowing that the Presence is there. Or in spiritual direction, when I and a friend touch on something so amazingly sacred and deep we are stunned into silence. We know in times like these that we exist, and that this existence is profoundly, intensely good.

This goodness is not limited to a certain way of life, such as the monastic calling, nor a certain religion or nation. It includes everything and refers to all, to the uncreated and the created, to God and to everything else. It includes our enemies. It is good that we are all here. Christian revelation, the Word spoken out of that abyss that God is, assures us of the goodness of our all being here. It is good that the mollusks bob about in the oceans; it is good that the maple leaves wave in the sun. It is good that each human being is, even as a person struggles and suffers and in spite of a person's vice. It is good that we are here.

Blessed Julian of Norwich wrote, "I saw in the same showing that if the blessed Trinity could have made man's soul any better, any more beautiful, any nobler than it was made, He would not have been wholly pleased with the creation of man's soul. But because He made man's soul as fair, as good, as precious a creature as He could make it, therefore the Blessed Trinity is wholly pleased without end in the creation of man's soul, and He wills that our hearts be powerfully raised above the depths of the earth and all vain sorrows, and rejoice in Him" (*Lesson*, Chapter 68).

In spite of all the voices inside and outside of us that tell us *it's not good that you are here, you don't deserve to be, it would be better if you were not*, we can listen to the voice that loves us, that we discover in moments of profound beauty, love, and presence. This voice, this revelation of God's glory in us, says to us how wonderful it is that we are—that our sheer existence is part of the wondrous goodness of the being of all things from the mollusk in the ocean to the supernova in the skies, to God. We are enfolded in a goodness that loves all and celebrates and rejoices in the unity of all.

Hearing this word of love from God so deeply that it sings at the core of our being, some Christians are impelled to give themselves in the service of the poor or to work for justice. Some teach, some preach, and some are priests; some become martyrs. It is all beauty and gift.

The contemplative way is also a way of marveling response and surrender to this revelation of God's goodness. It is a way of being with this unfathomable goodness all our days and nights. Of course the mountain-top experiences always pass, as Peter was the first to find out. We can't build booths for ourselves to live always at that exalted height. (Someone who is always falling in love is likely to need therapy very soon!) But what the peak experience does for contemplative souls is to make us keenly aware of any last piece of negativity that is opposed to this all-encompassing joy. We then are compelled, by the inner force of conviction and love, to practice the art of surrendering all that is negative, wrathful, and resistant in ourselves in order to yield ourselves more completely to the divine rejoicing that is the reality of all things. As we spend the rest of our lives letting go of anything that is not of God, anything that resists the vision we have once seen, we become more and more open to its transfiguring light even as we go about our humblest duties.

⟶ LENT

L ENT IN THE MONASTERY is a time of self-reflection and renewed spiritual seriousness. There is more silence, more spiritual reading and prayer, and we abstain from our usual noon meal. We prepare ourselves during Lent to enter emotionally and spiritually into our Lord's Passion in Holy Week and to receive the gift of his Resurrection at Easter.

The meditations included in this section are the most detailed in this book. They reflect on the "deadly sins" of the Christian desert tradition, taken up and applied to the inner life of the contemplative with the help of two great saints, John Cassian and John of the Cross.

Reforming outward behavior, we discover, is only the beginning of the total conversion of life we are called to. Much more subtle and demanding is the work of purifying our inner world of attachments and desires that reveal an underlying self-centeredness even in our most spiritual intentions. Some of these sins have roots so deep that we cannot pull them out by ourselves; all we can do is to be aware of them, and in that awareness ask God to do the work.

⮜ The Middle Realm ⮞

I T WOULD BE PLEASANT TO THINK that the spiritual life
consisted of only two dimensions: the first being concern
with outward behavior and the second being a concern with our
inner, or spiritual, lives. But anyone who has ever tried to live
into contemplative presence or unceasing prayer knows that,
between outward behavior and contemplative experience, there
is a vast middle region of ourselves to be negotiated and purified.
This middle region is partly interior and partly exterior. It is the
region of our emotions, imaginations, and judgments. Lent is
an ideal time in the year to focus on these areas of our lives.

The Desert Fathers and Mothers expended great effort to
understand how to navigate this realm, how to bring peace and
healing there, so that the kingdom of God could flourish in
their hearts. They understood that reforming outward behavior
is only the first very small step toward union with God. The
majority of our labor is spent on bringing the middle realm of
thoughts and imaginations and feelings to a state of peace and
clarity so that God's light can indeed shine in and through us.

In the reflections that follow, I draw frequently on the teachings of St. John of the Cross (from the first book of *The Dark
Night*)[2] and John Cassian (from his *Institutes*).[3] You will notice
that I occasionally refer to John Cassian simply as Cassian, and
John of the Cross as John.

⌢ Lust: ⌢
Sexuality in Prayer

ALL THINGS AND PERSONS AND ALL OF CREATION can be imagined as existing in a golden field of energy. We could even say that we all exist together as a golden field of energy. This field is not static, but a living flow and a weaving that makes up reality.

Even if we can't name this golden field of energy that is existence, we do from time to time experience it. When we experience authentic tenderness, or beauty, we become conscious of ourselves as one with this woven fabric of Being. We know in that moment that we are a part of this weaving, this song, and this light.

At the same time, we also know from experience that when we behave viciously, we tear a hole in this Fabric. We create a painful dissonance in the Song. This is what sin is. Our response to our own sin is most often fearful and self-justifying. We retreat into coarseness, stubbornness, and self-righteousness. We get hard and hateful, proud and defensive. We begin to experience ourselves, as the existentialist philosophers noted, as a "tear in the fabric of Being." Hatred, anger, and despair all grow in us. A lot of culture is the attempt to live in this tear, and even to glorify this violence.

When we reflect on the need to take care of our mental and emotional worlds—what I have called the "middle realm" of the spiritual life—we do so in the awareness that our tendency to wound true reality and to isolate ourselves from its flow begins in our thoughts, even if they are half-formed, and in our instinctive habits of body and mind. This is why Jesus tells us that we commit adultery even when we think or look lustfully at another. Likewise, one who calls his brother "fool," Jesus says, deserves hellfire. In saying this Jesus was not trying to be a moralist cracking down on wayward sinners and hypocrites. He was trying to make us aware of the harm we do to ourselves even by our most secret and private thoughts.

Such an awareness is especially important when we reflect on sexual morality and the need to work consciously with our sexual imaginations and desires. Even if a majority of Christians are doing OK with sexuality in terms of outward actions, the inward mental and emotional "middle realm" of sexual thoughts, imaginations, and desires remains a painful and difficult area for most of us. This in turn is what makes us fearful, self-righteous, and judgmental of others in matters of outward sexual behavior. This is why we long for scapegoats in these matters. We long for someone who is clearly "other" than the majority in which we find ourselves, onto whom we can cast the unconscious anxiety and shame that is generated by our secret problems.

When we on the contemplative way reflect on the sin of lust, we are not talking about actual physical unchastity—actually breaking our marriage or monastic vows. We are talking rather about the much more common experience of wandering thoughts, emotions, imaginations, and the disturbing inner arousal we experience as a result of all this. We are looking carefully and with great compassion at our experience of unin-tegrated sexual energy that makes it difficult for us to live in our truest reality. Our ability to release ourselves to the Flow of Being that is God and all things is limited or blocked by unintegrated sexual energy. When it has not been consciously integrated and understood in our lives, this energy can become angry or disturbing.

For me, it is once again Julian of Norwich who provides a most helpful understanding of the ground of true chastity. She says in the first showing of her *Revelations of Divine Love* that we are not to seek our rest in any creature. If we do seek our rest or home in any creature, we are bound to be frustrated, restless, and eventually filled with wrath. While this desire to find rest in another creature extends beyond the emotional and physical desires related to sexuality, it certainly includes our sexuality and situates it within the basic human desire for wholeness.

John of the Cross, in his examination of unchaste thoughts, images, and arousal in lives already given to God, sees three different sources for these thoughts (*Dark Night*, I.4). First, he says that when our spirit enters deeply into prayer, sometimes some of the energy of the prayer flows over from our spirit into our sensual nature. If we do not consent to these "inner movements" (as he calls them) there is no harm done to ourselves or the fabric of being. We are still flowing with the One, and united with the many. But if we consent to them, and choose them, that's when the harm happens. Such arousal from prayer is for John a sign that we are perhaps still too attached to our sensual way of experiencing reality.

The second source of sexual thoughts and arousal, according to John, is the devil, who inserts them into our life of prayer to make modest persons afraid of prayer and to discourage us from continuing in it. John has in mind here the experience of something or someone becoming a cause of sexual thoughts while we are, for instance, at Eucharist or in contemplative prayer. The harm of this, if it causes us to flee from Eucharist or prayer, is obvious.

Third, and amazingly, John says that a third source of erotic imaginations and arousal is our own fear of them! This is an incredible psychological insight. The idea is that our fear of sexuality is itself a repressive obsession with sexuality. Instead of our sexual energy flowing naturally through our bodies as energizing and creative power in our work and play, we stamp this energy down into the unconscious, from which it breaks forth unexpectedly and with disturbing power. Surely John is writing out of his own experience and reflection.

In an interesting side-comment, John says that those who are temperamentally more inclined to melancholy (and by "melancholy" he means more moodiness than what we call clinical depression) will have greater problems with lustful thoughts and more difficulty with their sexuality. All of this John unfolds with great skill and upfront honesty, not to show how bad we are, but to make us aware of the normality of these experiences and of how they can be given to God for purification.

From John's analysis we can take courage. We can assume that as we journey deeper into prayer, we might well experience sexual thoughts and images rising up into consciousness. We need not be horrified at this, but neither should we become obsessed with it. It is best instead to regard it as so much news—stuff passing by in the stream of consciousness. We neither cling to nor repress it, but observe and allow it to pass through. We let it go to Jesus. We work on chastening our moodiness. We make friends with our sexual energy and invite it into the whole of our day.

When we go from John of the Cross to John Cassian, we are moving to a much more primitive but still very experienced strata of our spiritual tradition.

Cassian wanders around a great deal in his attempt to address the problem of "the spirit of fornication." For him, unchastity in thoughts, desires, emotions, and imaginings could only be dealt with if we have first dealt with our gluttony. The two are so interrelated for Cassian that it is useless to expect to be chaste if we are overindulging at the table. If we haven't learned moderation and temperance in our habits of eating, Cassian says, we will never be able to deal with the spirit of fornication. This is in fact a universal teaching that comes to us directly from the experience of the first contemplatives in the desert: what you do with eating will greatly affect what happens with your sexuality.

Cassian also understands that for many of us the struggle with inner chastity will be lifelong. The stories from the Desert Fathers are full of incidents that reinforce this opinion. Wayward emotions and thoughts will be with us for a long time. For some of us, these may have more of a relational and emotional nature; for others they will be more directly physical.

Cassian sees authentic chastity, the purification and transformation of our erotic drive, as one of the greatest gifts of the spiritual life, allowing a special purity of insight and openness to God. I am charmed by Cassian's belief that in the end it is humility before God that allows for disturbing and anarchic sexual energy to be, not repressed, but yielded to God and made to be the very energy by which we engage our prayer. In humility, we accept that our wayward thoughts are telling us something about ourselves and we ask Jesus to show us how we might address these issues. In Cassian, as in John of the Cross, the main advice is to learn to be aware of our sexuality, its energy in all our desires, and to offer this new energy to God for God's work in the world.

When we, as contemplatives, make the effort to become fully conscious of the flow and force of our sexuality, we are part of the healing of the sexual pain that is in our Church and culture. We are choosing to make ourselves like windows that allow the light and fresh air of consciousness into a dark, narrow room of repression, shame, and fear. On the other hand, we become a part of this problem if we repress sexual energy and hide behind a pious facade or if we allow ourselves to be possessed by the "spirit of fornication" to the detriment of our reality and that of others.

Gluttony:
Eating Too Much at God's Table

IN THE TRADITIONAL LISTING OF seven or eight types of sin, gluttony (or excessive appetite and delectation) can come after or before lust. The two are intimately related and cannot be dealt in isolation from each other. Although overeating is itself a huge problem in the developed world, our reflections on gluttony will be focused less on outward behavior and more on an inordinate appetite for pleasing spiritual knowledge, feelings, and experiences. This gluttony of the spirit can be most disabling to contemplatives seeking union with God.

In *The Dark Night*, John of the Cross has a great deal to say about spiritual gluttony (*Dark Night*, I.6). John understands spiritual gluttony as an infantile attachment to spiritual pleasures and experiences—what we would call "good feelings." He observes how this leads many people into disobedience and recklessness in their lives. While spiritual gluttony can be attached to ordinary pleasures of prayer and communion, he also notes that it can also be an inverted and masochistic attachment to suffering, mortification, and penance. In this inverted gluttony people are harsh on themselves beyond the custom of their community because of the sense of pride, accomplishment, or pleasure it gives them. As St. Paul wrote, such mortifications "have indeed an appearance of wisdom in promoting self-imposed piety, humility and severe treatment of the body, but they are of no value in checking self-indulgence" (Colossians 2:23). John says of people in a state of spiritual gluttony of whatever kind: "If they do not get what they want, they become sad and go about like testy children." He says that "they are weak and remiss in treading the rough way of the Cross. A soul given up to pleasure naturally feels aversion toward the bitterness of self-denial." Whenever we are seeking inner feelings of delight and sweetness, we have ceased to follow Christ. Instead of an overheated spirituality, John wants to lead us into an enormous freedom of spirit characterized by surrender, equanimity, and peace. John says that God purges us of our fault of spiritual gluttony by giving us trials, temptations, and aridity.

A way forward, out of material and spiritual gluttony, is by learning to connect, in contemplative prayer or in the practice of mindfulness in ordinary life, with that depth of self where we are always, already one with God. In our contemplative prayer, we set aside even our desires for spiritual feelings or consolations. We practice letting go of the obsessive hungers of the egoistic mind in order to let the eternal blossom through us. Connecting with our eternal depth, allowing it to expand into our daily consciousness, we are less driven to stuff "foods" into ourselves or to be harsh against ourselves. We come to be at home with ourselves as persons already open to experience the flow of God's life in us. Grabbing at things, devouring foods or experiences or knowledge, or being harsh with ourselves, is then completely beside the point.

⌒ Greed: ⌒
Selfish Monks and Mystics

I N THE DESERT TRADITION, the struggle with avarice, or greed, follows after lust and gluttony. This was a special problem for the earliest monks because, having at the start minimal communal organization, each monk had control over his or her resources. Reading the stories from the monastic desert gives the impression that these first monks were both surprised and horrified at finding greed still inhabiting their souls and being so much a part of their lives. Even after they had renounced the world and journeyed into the desert wastelands (and for some of them this meant renouncing lives of lavish luxury and political power), they still found themselves troubled by a desire to maintain a private store of personal wealth. While the experience of desert monks hiding little bags of copper coins in their cells may seem amusing and remote from our own struggles with greed in our consumerist age, John Cassian's reflections on the psychological root of greed, as experienced by the first desert monks, have a lot to teach us.

In his attempt to better understand the wiles of greed for the monks and nuns living in primitive monastic community, Cassian fictionalized a first-person monologue of the avaricious monk in Book Seven of his *Institutes*.

The avaricious thoughts begin, Cassian says, with the fear of prolonged illness and old age. The relevance of this anxiety to our age's problem with greed is immediate and obvious. The fear of not being provided for in the case of a prolonged illness, says Cassian, drives the monk to build up a private fund of money, hidden from his abbot and built up by overwork or dishonest means or by selling the products of his work at an unfairly high price. The monk then becomes increasingly obsessed with the thought of having more and more in his private fund. Nothing is ever enough. His greed makes him more deceptive and duplicitous and drives him to increasing excesses of overwork. All this stress, which is really anxious self-concern and the shame of hypocrisy, bursts out of the monk in the form of discontent with everything, a profound disgust with what is. The monk becomes unwilling to do the common work and is judgmental of others. He becomes an outsider in his own community, unwilling to live as others live, is lying and disobedient, and is filled with wrath and hidden shame.

In this analysis, Cassian shows us how a deep, unconscious drive for security causes fear and distrust, a malaise of discontent combined with anxious overwork that alienates us from the flow of life in the human community. Moreover, shame in our own hypocrisy causes us to be judgmental of others and to despise life with others.

John of the Cross, centuries later, reflected on avarice in a largely spiritualized mode, as either a greed for religious things or a greed for special experiences (*Dark Night*, I.3).

He notes how people can become greedy for religious or spiritual items—icons and relics, rosaries and paintings, and so forth. Because these are religious in content, it seems acceptable to want them badly, and to be attached to them once we have them. But John insists that these outward things should not preoccupy the soul. We have to cut through to the substance of devotion, which John of the Cross describes as "striving after mortification and the perfection of the interior poverty to which we are called." We can become preoccupied in our thoughts with holy things—liking more our possession of them than the relationship with God in interior nakedness that might be mediated through them. Instead of walking out into true poverty before the living God, we can content ourselves with managing a warehouse of delightful spiritual knickknacks, books, and icons. Here we find the same old desire for security sneaking in, through a greed for things to identify with.

Beyond this material aspect of spiritual greed, John also touches on the problem of being avaricious for religious ideas, thoughts, and counsels, rather than simply applying the few we actually need to achieve perfection in loving God and our neighbor. This is something we run into a great deal in the committed Christian life. We are content to fill our hearts and minds with whole libraries of inspiring or beautiful thoughts rather than actually practicing the one or two basic mortifications that would transform us. We avoid God by continuously feeding a welter of fancy religious ideas in ourselves. Many people seem content to collect superficial bits and pieces from any spiritual tradition they run across, making for themselves an ultimately evasive and delusive pastiche of ideas and inspirations. Such superficial collecting allows us to avoid God and the demands of engaging with God.

John Cassian and John of the Cross did not live in the consumeristic and materialistic societies of today. Their concerns may seem quaint in the face of the seductions of the marketplace that continuously challenge our souls today. But look at what happens when we combine their two reflections on avarice: John was concerned with the avarice that builds up a spirituality that is in reality a fearful evasion of the living God and of the naked poverty one needs in order to live in God's presence. Cassian gives us a picture of a monk who, similarly, is driven by fear and distrust to separate himself from the common life of the community. Combining these two, we have a searching analysis of the problems that contemplative spirits will face in everyday life.

Our need for security will drive us to be overly concerned about worldly goods and possessions. This will separate us from others and we will begin to feel ourselves as existing in competition with everyone and everything. For those who belong to religious communities, it is tempting to cloak our individual need for security in an unconscious, powerful greed for the community (if not ourselves) to have more and more wealth. When greed grows and begins to dominate our lives, we grow hard and cold and closed off from the flow of what is true reality in God. We become isolated units, and God and religion are at best secondary and superficial ideas we stick on from the outside to make us feel better about ourselves.

Even in our search for deeper spirituality, more connectedness to God, our primitive need for emotional security will drive us to hoard a variety of spiritual or religious objects, from material things and books to imaginations and ideas. We center our religion not on the encounter with the risen Christ in poverty and nakedness of spirit, but in a more comfortable realm of using ideas to give us feelings of self-worth, self-importance, or moral superiority. We even cling greedily to any spiritual consolations we are given, any insights or experiences, because they bolster our sense of being someone unique.

The end of such greediness is just as Cassian describes, that we live more and more as isolated, fearful beings, hoarding goods, being duplicitous, judgmental, and condemning about what is. We apparently have more stuff, yet our disgust and our fearfulness only increases.

What might be the remedy? Cassian advised his monks and nuns to be strong and renounce any desire to have anything other than what the community provides. They are to cut off greed at the very root—the fear of not being provided for in illness and old age. John would, I think, agree with this counsel for active renunciation; but he combines it with a more passive approach in which one suffers the loss of the very things one is greedy for. God weans us from spiritual greed simply by denying us any consolation, any feeling of connection in spiritual things. We suffer a passive purification of our soul's greed as an experience of an inner aridity for religious and spiritual matters, even as we remain totally committed to God. By this we are weaned from anything other than the intention to be God's in utter nakedness of spirit.

Practically speaking, very few of us belong to religious communities. We cannot throw ourselves on the mercy of the communal life and finances and renounce any worrisome thought about the future. But what anyone can do is:

1. Take the time in prayer to make appropriate plans for a modest future, recognizing that illness and death will remain a part of life no matter what we do with our money.

2. Give some of our money away on a regular and self-sacrificial basis. We are called to tithe as Christians out of loving compassion for our brothers and sisters, but also because it allows us to maintain a fresh and clean spirit. It is perhaps the most potent and necessary tool that we, especially in the developed world, can use against greed.

Ultimately, the only thing that works with greed is the only thing that works in the rest of our struggle in the middle realm of thoughts and imaginations that separate us from God: vigilant awareness of what is, in fact, going through our heads and dwelling emotionally in our bodies. Practice the art of surrendering your anxious self-concern to God, over and over and over again—whether it is concern for security, power, or affection. When our obsessive thoughts are circling around these needs, our bodies are tight with emotions of fear and anxiety, but by holding these in awareness, we gradually come to the place of letting them go. Awareness is itself healing and creative.[4]

Anger:
Intoxicating Power

ACCORDING TO CASSIAN, THE FOURTH STRUGGLE to be engaged in the desert tradition is with the passion of anger. More than anyplace else, Cassian appears to be speaking here out of direct personal experience.

How we live with anger, recognize its harm, and open it to healing is bound to be a sensitive issue. Anger is our attempt to make ourselves feel safe. It is our way of flaring up defensively against a reality that seems, rightly or wrongly, to threaten us. Thus even suggesting that we should let go of habitual anger, the anger that we have identified with, will likely make us feel vulnerable or unsafe. Also, giving up our anger can seem threatening because anger, with its hard denunciation of others, is a way we use to build up a faltering identity or self-worth.

Anger is intoxicating because while it lasts it appears to bestow on us a kind of unassailable righteousness, a strong and clearly defined self—it gives us an inflated sense of being bigger than we are, bigger than others and reality itself, central in fact to reality, and morally on God's side. Thus, whether our anger is expressed in a flaring temper or sullen withdrawal and resentment, we are using the anger in order to feel safe or build up an identity.

Cassian's overriding concern is that the monk or nun be left with no valid grounds for arguing that anger is justified. He wants first to expose the destructive reality of anger by disallowing any possibility that it is a good or godly thing. To back this up, he cites the experience of the elders of the desert, the words of Jesus, and St. Paul's different admonitions about anger. Cassian says that anger makes us blind to God's reality, causes us to lose wisdom, discretion, and our purity of mind, and makes it impossible for the Holy Spirit to dwell in us. Anger also destroys any chance we might have of creatively addressing and transforming what made us angry in the first place. This last insight is very helpful. If we really want to change a situation, and some situations desperately need intervention and change, approaching the situation or person with an angry spirit (in reality, overcompensating for fear) is the least helpful thing we can do.

Besides discussing the negative effects of anger, Cassian is eager to point out that solitude is no solution to the problem, because the root of anger is in us not in other people or other things. The first thing to be learned about anger in the monastic tradition is that it's more about ourselves than anything outside ourselves. Even if we go off into complete solitude, Cassian says, we will still find ourselves being angry and hating the pencil we are trying to write with. Thus, we don't respond to anger first off by striking out at what apparently caused the anger, as if just changing everything around us to our liking would take care of our problem with anger. Rather, it is something we must first become aware of and heal in ourselves. In a passage so strikingly modern that it could have come from Thomas Merton, Cassian writes:

> Sometimes, when we have been overcome by pride or impatience and are unwilling to correct our unseemly and

undisciplined behavior, we complain that we are in need of solitude, as if we would find the virtue of patience in a place where no one would bother us, and we excuse our negligence and the causes of our agitation by saying that they stem not from our own impatience but from our brothers' faults. But, as long as we attribute our own wrongdoing to other people, we shall never be able to get near to patience and perfection. The sum total of our improvement and tranquility, then, must not be made to depend on someone else's willing, which will never be subject to our sway; it comes rather, under our own power. And so our not getting angry must derive not from someone else's perfection, but from our own virtue, which is achieved not by another person's patience but by our own forbearance. (*Institutes*, Eight.16–17)

John of the Cross, for his part, addresses the imperfection of anger in spiritual beginners in the first book of *The Dark Night*. With his usual brevity and precision he identifies three areas of anger in beginners.

The first cause of anger represents John's frequent concern with how we behave once we have lost all our initial delight in spiritual exercises. He writes, "When the delight and satisfaction procured in their spiritual exercises passes, these beginners are naturally left without any spiritual savor. And because of this distastefulness, they become peevish in the works they do and easily angered by the least thing, and occasionally they are so unbearable that nobody can put up with them" (*Dark Night*, I.5.1).

There are times in our lives of prayer when God appears to withdraw and we are left with only a sense of absence, or personal pettiness, or spiritual failure, or aridity and meaninglessness. Because our life is rooted in a more infantile desire to get what we crave, rather than to give ourselves away for love, we often respond with a kind of childish testiness to all of life when the spiritual dries up. This kind of fault can only be healed by the long purification of the dark nights, where we learn faith and love.

Second, John sees beginners becoming angry with others for their sins. He says that when we are beginners we are likely to set ourselves up as "lords of virtue" who are tempted to correct others aggressively. That this is itself a great fault, and that correcting another in anger never works, Cassian himself took note of, citing the Gospel parable of the mote and the beam.

Finally, John sees beginners being so eager for perfection that they live in a constant state of anger with themselves for not being better. In this last case, spiritual perfection is something they want for themselves and are upset when they can't get it. This leads them to make all kinds of resolutions and yet fail to keep any of them and so get more angry. John is touching here on a phenomenon that is very important for us to see clearly: if we are living the spiritual life for our own ego's sake, we will always be frustrated and angry with ourselves when we fall short, and we will engage in the false behavior of making resolutions as a way of avoiding the self-knowledge presented in our failings. We are using the spiritual life for building up our own ego, so we get angry when we aren't what we want to be, and we identify with the new resolve rather than with the sin. Making resolutions, in this light, is a way of perpetuating falsehood.

We actually have to want to heal our own habits of anger. We have to want to grow in humility, meekness, patience—and we want these things for the sake of prayer, for being able to live with God, live in the kingdom. If we don't want this, if we want to cling to our anger, then there is no possibility for growth.

Unfortunately, neither Cassian nor John gives us much practical help in dealing with the anger that we have, and how we go about offering it to healing. Cassian simply warns us of how destructive it is; John insists (to my mind correctly) that this fault is only cured by the secret work of God in purifying us from our basic self-concern and selfishness.

In the long term, what frees us from our anger, as with gluttony, is our growing experience of an eternal depth inside of ourselves, what Mother Julian calls our "soul's substance," and this we experience in our disciplines of prayer and mindfulness. Our temporal selves, our egotistical modes of consciousness, what Julian calls our "sensuality," are by definition fearful and needy, and this is the source of the anger. The more we touch on our eternal self, the more our temporal, fearful, needy self becomes like a radio playing in the background. It is still there, and we still have flashes of anger, but we are not obsessed or possessed by them. Anger is just background noise, and our soul easily recovers its natural equilibrium because we are living from a different ground than our frightened selves. From both Julian and John I get a sense that our anger is only healed by our getting in touch with our eternal self in its naked openness to God.

In the short term, we have the responsibility of bringing our experiences of anger before God, unfolding them before grace, giving them room and space to breathe without being possessed by them. We walk a middle road. We neither repress our anger (which only makes us sick in the end), nor do we indulge in it by a persistent habit of playing the angry thoughts in our head, or living in resentment, or withdrawing in sullen gloom from others. We rather take the matter before God.

As Christians, the best place to take anger is before our crucified Lord. It is after all Jesus in his Passion who slakes our wrath and reconciles us to the eternal joy of God. When anger goes beyond a flash, and develops into a habitual attitude, we take this before our Lord in his Passion, lay it out before him, talk to him about it, and tell him how we feel. In my experience this can bring real healing and transformation, even if it takes a great deal of time.

Your anger is telling you something very important about yourself. It is like a flag waving above a part of your life that needs to be looked at and consciously opened to grace. Do not repress the anger, and avoid as much as you can indulging in it, but explore what it means, and what it is saying about your life.

⌒ *Sadness:* ⌒
The Smoking of Damped-Down Wrath

I<small>N</small> C<small>ASSIAN'S</small> <small>CATALOG OF DESERT STRUGGLES</small>, the struggle with sadness follows on anger. Sadness, he says, often comes after anger as a form of the anger itself. Sadness can come when something injurious happens to us from outside, or from apparently no cause at all—from what he calls "an irrational turn of mind!" All of these are familiar to me and I expect to all of us.

Sadness and anger are two similar responses to reality. Where anger flares up against something, sadness withdraws into itself, but in essence they are both protests or defenses against things as they are. We are not OK with what is, we are unable to affirm or be open to it. Sometimes the cause is obvious and external—I am sad because I have been injured by a friend or overcome by a rival; I am sad because my plans did not work out. Sometimes the reason is hidden deep within us—a traumatic experience from childhood that makes the world seem unsafe or unworthy or unenjoyable.

Given the way life is, it is no wonder that sadness and anger are a part of our lives. Nothing can be more cloying than the simplistic belief that Christians should simply make themselves happy all the time. While it is unhelpful to lose our minds to sadness to a degree that leads to "deadly despair," as Cassian calls it, it is also unhelpful to pretend that there is no sadness at all.

Cassian says that we are safe from sadness when "we are ever rejoicing at the sight of things eternal . . . and when we remain steadfast and are neither cast down by present events nor carried away by good fortune, viewing both as empty and soon to pass" (*Institutes*, Nine.13). The idea is that our treasure and our heart are in the eternity of heaven, where, as Jesus says, "thieves don't break in and steal." We have then a kind of equilibrium; our moods aren't defined by things happening to us because we have not identified ourselves with anything other than a focused intention to serve and love God. Julian of Norwich echoes this when she says,

When God Almighty had shown so plentifully and so fully of His goodness, I desired to know of a certain creature that I loved if it would continue in good living (which I hoped by the grace of God was begun). And in this particular desire, it seemed that I hindered myself, because I was not shown at this time. And then I was answered in my reason, as it were by a friendly go-between: "Take this generally, and see the graciousness of the Lord God as He reveals it to thee; for it is more honor to God for thee to see Him in all things than in any special thing." I agreed, and with that I learned that it is more honor to God to understand all things in general than to delight in anything in particular. And if I would do wisely following this teaching, not only would I be glad for nothing in particular, but also not greatly disturbed by any manner of thing, for all shall be well. The fullness of joy is to behold God in all. (*Lesson*, Chapter 35)

Julian herself was inclined to melancholy and despair about sin and the suffering of the world, but was challenged by God to surrender herself to God's rejoicing in all things.

In a similar way, John of the Cross sees our sadness coming from a fixation on our own will and desires, instead of surrender to God's will. He writes, "Many of these beginners want God to desire what they want, and they become sad if they have to desire God's will. They feel an aversion toward adapting their will to God's. Hence they frequently believe that what is not their will, or brings them no satisfaction, is not God's will, and, on the other hand, that if they are satisfied, God is too. They measure God by themselves and not themselves by God" (*Dark Night*, I.7.3). John offers us the choice between clinging to our own will, and thus fluctuating between happiness and sadness, or moving to a deeper joy through surrendering to God's will. Once again we come across the fundamental mantra of the spiritual life: letting go to God.

What are we to make of these spiritual traditions urging us to keep our sight on things eternal, to surrender to divine providence, to release ourselves to God's rejoicing in all things? How can we avoid reading these as a kind of violence against our own sense of emotional integrity? If we think about the counsels of the saints in this way, our sadness is likely to turn to anger against spiritual things and we compound the problem. How do we come to the kind of sadness that Cassian says is full of the gifts of the Holy Spirit and even has in it a kind of joy (*Institutes*, Nine.11)?

I suggest that we think about eternity, or the realm of God's will, not as a distant realm that we throw our mental selves toward to avoid sadness, but rather as the present moment. Eternity is Now. It is the Now. We find a much greater equilibrium of spirit when we step out of our limited self's obsession with past and future and engage in open surrender to the reality that is here and now, this present moment.

If we look at our experience of sadness, what we find is that it has two general components, a bodily-emotional component and a mental component. The bodily-emotional component means that we feel something in our bodies that we identify with sadness—a pressure in the forehead or behind the eyes, a tightness in the chest, a heaviness in the belly, or even an overall sense of exhaustion and listlessness. In themselves, these are simply bodily sensations. But if we pay attention to the mental component, what is running through our heads, what we discover is a stream of consciousness filled with thoughts that reinforce and deepen our sadness. We discover that we are thinking about how bad or how unfair the world is, or how ugly or empty are lives are. We may even have brooding thoughts of hatred for things as they are. These thoughts create more emotional, bodily feelings of sadness, and these feelings reinforce the thoughts in a vicious cycle. The whole world closes in on us, and we become the aching wound of sadness.

I have discovered that the most helpful spiritual practice is to separate the bodily, emotional component from the mental component and to bring my awareness down into the former, into the body. This becomes my principal work in my hour of solitary prayer and reflection when I am downcast. Instead of reinforcing the vicious cycle of sad thoughts and sad feelings, I break the cycle by stepping into the middle of it, regard all thoughts as distractions, and simply spend time being aware, being frankly curious about the *bodily sensation* of sadness as it wells up in me. This takes real courage. If we break the cycle between thoughts and feelings in this way, and face head-on the actual physical feelings of sadness, their oppressiveness is lightened, or at least the cycle becomes less vicious.

Obviously, it is incredibly helpful to have already in place a practice of spending some time every day being present to oneself and to God—a time for prayer. If our prayer time is filled by praying a Divine Office from the Church, we can still spend five minutes feeling the sadness in ourselves and then turn to the office. If our prayer time is meditation on Scripture, we can do likewise. If our prayer time is a silent meditation or is Centering Prayer or mindful breathing, we can spend that time of stillness and quiet simply being fully aware, without judgment, without wanting even to change anything, of the sadness in our bodies. Experience shows that judging and being too eager to change things only makes them worse. Awareness is enough. There are many excellent books on mindful breathing available, and this practice is most helpful in dealing with sadness.[5]

However we do it, when we become aware in an accepting, open way of the feelings of sadness in our bodies, we find that we neither repress nor indulge in the feelings. We are stepping thus deeply into an awareness of the Now and because we have no agenda to change the situation our only intention is to be aware of it. What we experience is that being deeply present to ourselves in this way is an act of appropriate love for ourselves, which allows us to turn the experience, the inner feelings, to God, to Jesus, in a gesture of loving openness to him.

I am not saying that, because we love Jesus, we are never going to be sad. Rather, the occasion of our sadness becomes something we enter deeply into and own, offering the experience in love to Jesus by an act of surrender. This in fact is what gets us through—not repression nor indulgence, but a mature choice for clear awareness and deeper relationship through the experience of suffering. The oppressive heaviness of the sadness is lifted, if only a little; the vicious cycle involving the thoughts is stilled for a moment and we feel in ourselves an opening and offering of this most intimate part of who we are to Another, to Jesus, to God. We feel God's life then coming into the sadness, enfolding it, and penetrating it with a healing light. We begin to learn that we can trust God, and that, at the same time, we don't have to be victims of our moods, but can consciously choose to engage them in ways that open the moods and so our deepest selves to others.

⌐ Sloth: ⌐
The Noonday Demon

IN THE WESTERN TRADITION, *acedia* (also referred to as sloth) and sadness were combined to become the mortal sin of despair. For Cassian sloth and sadness are still two different things. Generally speaking, sloth is more serious than sadness. Whereas sadness involves emotional pain and mental negativity, sloth is a profound spiritual death, a kind of total spiritual insensitivity and lack of care that comes on one not at the beginning but in the *middle* of a committed spiritual life.

Indeed, the Greek root of *acedia* means "to be without care, to be indifferent." Originally it referred to those who allowed their dead to go unburied—which meant, for the ancient Greeks, to have lost all respect for the living as well as the dead, for the divine as well as the human. At its root, sloth means to have lost a sense of the sacredness of things, the sacred potentiality and meaning of human life. It is a profound state of spiritual death.

In terms of monastic vocation, Cassian saw this spirit of sloth attacking the monks at noonday, that is, in the middle of their lives. We don't face this at the dawning of our vocation or the first stages in the spiritual life. Generally it is only after we have made a good start, after we have expended energy and time working with our thoughts and emotions and striving for the total gift of ourselves to God that sloth shows up. After we have struggled with gluttony, lust, and avarice, sadness and anger, then the spirit of sloth comes along to say that none of that work was worth anything. The voice speaking inside us says that all this spiritual work is a sham, that God is not interested, and that if we were honest with ourselves, we would just give it up. It can manifest itself in a kind of inner mockery that suggests that our lives spent in the desert with Jesus are really worth nothing after all. The core of the problem of sloth is when we've lost all connection to our vocation, to contemplation, and to union with God—it all becomes unreal. Therefore, any ascetic effort or discipline or solitude seems pointless.

Cassian's description of a monk in this state in the tenth book of his *Institutes* should be required reading for everyone seeking to grow in intimacy with God. When sloth comes to a monk, Cassian says that he will be unable to live in his cell or be happy in his solitude. He will either give way to sleep or he will bustle about visiting other monks and chatting. He will dream up wonderfully pious things that he could be doing elsewhere. He will think of all the people he could be helping with his wonderful projects if only he hadn't committed himself to a life of prayer. He will encourage others to leave the monastery even if he does not have the courage to do so. Cassian points out how brothers or sisters afflicted with acedia will often hold their own monastery disrespectfully, and scorn their brothers and sisters. What has died is the sense of the sacred calling to solitude and silence as being beneficial and redemptive. This has happened periodically in my life, when I have let the sadness behind it get completely out of control.

Julian, in Chapter 73 of her *Revelations*, specifies sloth as one of the two sins that most tempt those who have given themselves to the contemplative life. Although we normally think of sloth as having to do with listlessness and torpor, Julian chooses to identify it with the opposite, impatience. Rather than offering our lives to love and learning, we become gloomy and irritated with all the little things that befall us.

For those not in a monastery, sloth will manifest itself in intense busyness that refuses to take time for prayer, as well as in sheer laziness. We will become totally numb to the idea of practicing our spiritual commitment in the life-situation we are already in. Cynicism may rise up in us. Sloth will tell us that our contemplative practice and prayer and meditation have been worth nothing, that one should just get on with active good works or just forget the religious and spiritual life altogether.

All contemplatives, anyone on a lifelong journey into God, will suffer bouts of sloth, moods that come and go, fade and intensify. Ours is, after all, a lifelong journey, and part of that journey is the dismantling of romantic expectations that got us started but that were not realistic and so can't be sustained for the long haul.

The solution that the desert fathers suggest is to contradict sloth head on. This is a hard teaching, but a universal one: if we give way to sloth in order to ease its pressure on us, if we allow ourselves to behave according to the feelings of inner spiritual deadness, it will only get worse. This is experiential wisdom coming to us directly from those great ammas and abbas of the Egyptian desert who lived their whole lives out in that harsh solitude. It is advice confirmed in the experience of thousands of spiritual practitioners since then. If we leave our spiritual practice to find someone to chat with in order to ease the burden of sloth, or if we indulge in fantasies about all the good works we could be doing elsewhere, or if we indulge in obsessive, negative thoughts about the community we are in, our families, or our particular life situations—if we idealize states of life other than our own, or if we give in to physical torpor—these will only get worse, and drive us into deeper irritation and laziness, and cause us to be busybodies. Eventually we will lose our zeal and commitment to the contemplative journey.

Cassian's advice is simple: regardless of what we are feeling, we contradict the sloth directly by applying ourselves as best we can to the work at hand with attentiveness, thoroughness, and care. This work could be physical work, educational work, artistic work, or something else. We are not to look elsewhere for fulfillment. We go back to square one in each thing we do, and discover a wonderful, novice-like joy at starting over again with a good heart. In short, we move through sloth by deliberately stepping out of the negative thoughts in our heads, stepping over the draining torpor in our bodies, and engaging the duties and responsibilities that are directly at hand.

⌒ *Vanity:* ⌒
Telling God How Great You Are

I MAGINE THAT YOU HAVE BEEN GIVEN AN EVENING with the person you most love in the world. Then imagine that you spend the entire evening talking about all the things you would rather be doing! You drop names, you talk about the people you like to do things with, or you ramble on about all the things that others have done for or against you in years past.

It sounds crazy, but in our relationship with God, who is the One our souls most deeply long for, this is how most of us live our whole lives. Our Beloved is here offering communion in the present moment and yet we do everything we can not to be in this moment. We ignore the divine presence as we repel the present moment, living instead in past guilt and future anxiety and desire. And what we call our selves, what are really our false selves, are constituted by just this resistance to what is right here and now and longing for what is not yet here. Julian of Norwich calls this baseline of resistance "wrath." It is the very opposite of the loving openness and relationship that she calls "friendship." God is our blessed Friend, but we are so worried about how our lives are going to turn out that we don't open and yield and practice trust in God.

When we reflect on vanity we are reflecting on a core dynamic of the separated self, the self constituted by Julian's notion of "wrath." Because such a separated, false self—created by opposition rather than communion—has no ultimate reality, it must continuously work to create a positive reality for itself, and its chief means of doing this is through comparison with others and judgment against others. The false self is thus necessarily vainglorious; for its reality, it is dependent on how other people look at it. Because the false self has ceased to receive its sense of worth from the loving of God and the authentic loving and care for others, it tries to live on the feelings of being superior to others or in conflict with them. The false self is intensely fearful, judgmental, and competitive.

Precisely because this is such a constitutional need of the false self, it will use anything at all as a means to its advancement. This is what so puzzled Cassian: how vanity will use absolutely anything to puff itself up. The poor will use their poverty as a means of vanity as surely as the wealthy will use their wealth. The well-fed and healthy will use their health in this way, while the starving and ill will use their malnourishment or sickness. Those who oppress others will bloat themselves in their self-importance, while those who are victimized are often tempted to create a false self as perpetual victims. What is common in all these cases is that such people have stopped living from the richness of God's love and are seizing upon some aspect of current experience—it does not matter at all what that aspect is—and using this as a kind of weapon in order to feel they are better than others. Such an inner habit is not so much a sin that separates us from God as it is a symptom that we are already separated.

Cassian tells a lovely story about an elder coming up to a younger novice monk's cell, and hearing the young brother inside pretending that he is preaching at the Eucharist. Like a little boy pretending he is a sports star, the novice monk is so crazed for the admiration of others that he indulges in this fantasy world of pretense. And it goes on! When the novice finishes his fantasy sermon, he then switches his voice and pretends he is the deacon who is dismissing the catechumens. At this point, the elder knocks on the door. The young brother, afraid that the elder heard him in his fantasy, asks how long he had been there. The elder says, "I came along just as you were dismissing the catechumens!"

We can laugh at this; it seems harmless, and in some ways, it is very innocent. However, we often live in a negative fantasy world where we constantly tell ourselves mental stories that reinforce our scorn of others, our feelings of superiority or of dramatic opposition. Our false self lives out of the inner script always playing in our heads, about how we compare with others, about their faults or our gifts, how we are victims or heroes.

The first step toward healing is for us to be aware of our vanity—how it is a constant part of our stream of consciousness. When we find ourselves judging others, creating opposition with others, or relishing a sense of being more important than others, then we can be sure we are living in our false selves. We can afford to laugh at ourselves a little when we see how anxiously we go about trying to scrape together a sense of self by inflating ourselves in our own thoughts or judgments! We observe how our psyche loves being in conflict with someone, because the conflict seems to bestow on us a sense of reality and identity we would not have otherwise.

One observation that Cassian returns to again and again is that vanity is not really resolved by a direct refusal or contradiction; it simply mutates into something else. If we try to defeat it by making believe we are humble, we will likely start being judgmental of others for being so vain or proud. We all know how this works. The only solution is our gradual ability to stand in our true selves, our most transparent selves, that are constituted not by underlying resistance, vanity, and mental obsessiveness, but in pure responsiveness to God. And this is where spiritual direction or at least a spiritual friendship can be so valuable. As we sit with our spiritual friends and share with them all that fills our hearts and minds, they will likely try to see more clearly what is true and what is false in us. A spiritual friend, if skilled in these matters, will be able to pierce tactfully our vanity and our habit of judging others and call us back to living from a core identity of being loved in God.

John of the Cross would say that we have to go through the progressive series of *spiritual nights* in order to come to this kind of simplified, transparent, true self of presence in God's presence. I think he is right. But whether we think in terms of John's progression through ever-deeper levels of purification, or Benedict's idea of monastic life as a journey into humility, or Julian's vision of the mercy of God spreading outward from our essential depths, slaking our wrath and one-ing us to divine bliss, we are looking at the same process. This is the journey we are on; this is what is happening to us.

A great joy leaps up in the heart of God when God's people realize that surrender is what their lives are actually about— letting go of their agonized, vain, false selves so that the true simplicity of who they are can emerge. There are always so many things happening in our lives: there are so many things of beauty or ugliness, joy or sorrow, conflict or harmony, and we can be lured into the belief that these are what we are actually about. We can become combatants in a life defined by conflict. Yet when we open to life in surrender, we begin to realize instead that life is about our wedding with God. The lovely Friend is here and we can afford to let go of some of our fear, some of our vanity, and step out into the peace, humility, transparent simplicity that is here and now. At the end—oh, blessing of blessings—we stop talking about ourselves.

Pride:
Devil Be Damned!

I WAS TWENTY YEARS OLD WHEN I ARRIVED at the monastery, having wanted to be a monk since I was sixteen. I thought that I had prepared myself well for monastic life by studying theology and reading the most serious mystical texts. I was confident, as I walked through the front door into my new home, that I knew what the spiritual life was about, and I had had some spiritual experiences to prove that I really knew how to live spiritually. This means, of course, that I started judging and was trying to teach others even before I had been clothed in the monastic habit.

I can smile at that behavior now. It is, in a way, age-appropriate, and in the least reveals a seriousness of intention. But looking back, I can see clearly how I was filled with pride, and that this pride was driven by deep fear and insecurity. Afraid of others and unsure of myself, I built an unassailable tower of intellectual and spiritual pride from which I could peer down, and judge others, and offer my thoughts.

John Cassian, in his discussion of pride, does not add much to the preceding discussion on vanity, except to say that vanity is a little more innocent than pride, a little less damnable. Pride has a harder, more vicious, more of a devil-be-damned attitude. Cassian does, however, offer a colorful description of the proud monk. The proud monk will be suspicious of spiritual conferences, and so hyper-critical of anyone who tries to teach spiritually. He is puffed up with himself. His speech is unguarded, loud and glib. He will be prone to irrational moods, and will hold the discipline of the community in disgust. He will even blame his lack of progress or lack of holiness on the community around him. This is such an accurate picture of me as a novice monk that it makes me wince!

John of the Cross is something of a comfort to me, because he says that such spiritual pride is normal, almost to be expected, in spiritual beginners. Once we begin to know God, we tend to use this knowledge, he says, not to love others more sacrificially, but to puff ourselves up and dominate others. John writes that such beginners, having experienced just a little of God, become complacent in themselves and "develop a desire somewhat vain—at times very vain—to speak of spiritual things in others' presence, and sometimes even to instruct rather than be instructed; in their hearts they condemn others who do not seem to have the kind of devotion they would like them to have, and sometimes they give expression to this criticism like the pharisee who despised the publican" (*Dark Night*, I.2.1). John goes on to say how pride leads spiritual beginners to speak poorly of others and to be dishonest with their spiritual directors. Instead of using the experience of their faults to grow in humility and self-knowledge, they get impatient and start hating themselves for their faults. Their spiritual life is about wanting to maintain a certain image, a certain spiritual greatness for themselves. Thus, instead of a tranquil openness to reality, relationship, and growth, they flip back and forth between overbearing pride in relation to others when they think they are doing well, and impatience with themselves leading to pointless self-condemnation when they feel they have performed poorly.

This kind of spiritual pride can be as much a problem for people practicing a contemplative life in the world as in a monastery. Its modality may shift a little, but basically the same problem of looking down on others in other walks of life, being judgmental, full of oneself, and at root simply being terrified of relationship and of being vulnerable to others is the same for all of us.

The most illuminating word of advice coming from Cassian and the desert tradition is a signaling of gratitude as the key mark of humility and so the opposite of pride. We can keep ourselves safe from pride by practicing gratitude for the unimaginably wonderful gifts that are given to us every day: the gift of the other amazing people in our lives, the gift of food and clean water, the gift of employment and community, and the gift of a spiritual tradition that feeds and nurtures us. Gratitude is not a spontaneous feeling that sometimes pops up in us; it is a habit that we can practice and learn, by looking for the small, wonderful, pleasurable, meaningful things in life, and being grateful for them. As we grow strong in this practice, we learn to apply it to things that are neutral and even unpleasant. Our hearts begin to be open to the reality of what we are given as the means of God's presence with us and our surrender to him. Cassian says that the grateful nun or monk is eager to learn from others, is modest in speech and behavior, moves along carefully and attentively through the day, takes up the disciplines of the rule of life as a way to God, and reveres those around her. We could say that gratitude, gentleness, and tender presence to others are all expression of the contemplative life running deeply in a person.

If the life of divine intimacy, and of contemplative conversion, is anything at all, it is an invitation to humility, which is to say, an invitation to gratitude, openness, simplicity, presence, and peace. I know from my own life in the monastery that what helped to break my proud patterns was learning how to accept the love of others. In fits and starts I slowly began to experience other people not as threats or challenges, but as people who would hold me in love and genuinely care for my good—who suffered when I suffered and rejoiced when I grew even just a little into God's joy. I began to realize I did not need my unassailable tower of pride, but that I could walk out into the open plane where I could meet people as genuine friends, and celebrate the gift of our common life together. At that point, I stopped needing to judge and condemn so much. Even my moods moderated. I learned that I was safe with others and even, in this new security of love, that I could help others to grow in love in this same way.

⟶ EASTER

EASTER IS THE MOST IMPORTANT SEASON in the monastery's life—in the Christian life. The Easter proclamation of Jesus' bodily resurrection, following the dark solemnity of Good Friday and the emptiness of Holy Saturday, rises like the first rays of dawn after a dark night, announcing our deliverance from fear, anxiety, and death.

In the monastery, Easter is celebrated with the greatest festivities of the year, beginning with the three-hour Great Vigil service on the night before Easter. For all fifty days of Easter, the meals are a little more lavish, and the brothers and sisters are invited to spend more time in creative and artistic ventures.

Easter is not merely a celebration of light returning after darkness, or spring returning after winter. It is not about the cyclical renewal of life, but Jesus' bodily resurrection breaking completely through the cycles of life and offering eternal life to us, now, in our bodies. The Resurrection disturbs almost every assumption we hold about the physical world, our bodies, and our lives and deaths, inviting us into a life so unexpected and new that it takes months and years to get used to.

The meditations in this section begin with reflections on Easter that are followed by meditations on Ascension and Ascensiontide. The section comes to end with a meditation on the contemplative meaning of Pentecost.

Hearing Our Name

I N THE THE STORY OF EASTER MORNING in John's Gospel, St. Mary of Magdala is an image of contemplative life. St. Peter (considered the image of church authority) runs to the tomb, jumps in, jumps out, and runs away, too eager to start talking about Christ to encounter the risen Lord. Theological authority, represented by St. John, follows Peter into the tomb, and follows Peter out again as he runs away. But Mary, who wants her Lord with her whole heart, soul, mind, and strength, simply stays at the tomb weeping until she encounters him.

At first, Mary does not recognize the risen Christ. She thinks he is the gardener. But then he says her name, "Mary," and she suddenly knows who he is. He is the Teacher, and she falls before him in total devotion.

Most of us live through the delights and crises of ordinary life, its joys and insights, plans and frustrations, without much sense of God being around. Certainly we do not live our life in ecstasies. In particularly difficult times, when life seems like a wreckage of lost hopes and aspirations, we weep for God in what seems like his absence, his death. We are like Mary Magdalene weeping at the tomb. But then Jesus calls us by our true name and we turn to behold his presence. In seeing and knowing him, we know ourselves to be utterly and completely his. We cling to him. We cleave to him.

If our contemplative lives have some strictness to them, some necessary emptiness and even loneliness, it is because we need to nurture our desire to cling to the resurrected presence of our

Lord as the very meaning of our vocation. There is so much that can lead us away from him into a dissipation of spirit. But having heard him utter our own eternal name, we know that we want to be entirely his, without conditions.

This uttering of our eternal name does not usually happen with words, but in a depth beyond words, in the silence that is an expression of our longing for God at the center of our grief. Perhaps during our morning meditation, perhaps in the middle of a busy day, perhaps as we lie in bed at night, we know ourselves to be in the presence of the Holy One, our Lord. And we know that he desires our love. We know that we are his. The essential thing is not to run away from the tomb of ordinary life, where God seems to have died, but to stay there, weeping inwardly or outwardly, until he comes and speaks.

Nothing Matters Except
to Be with Him

WHEN WE WAKE UP IN THE MORNING and lie in bed listening as the house comes to life, when we are out weeding the vegetable garden, sweat trickling down our arms, when we are writing letters to friends or driving to the store, we can stop what we are doing and repeat to ourselves the strange, disturbing, and wonderful news: Alleluia. Christ is Risen. The Lord is Risen indeed. Alleluia.

It is strange, disturbing, and wonderful news: the tomb where his body was laid is empty. Nothing like this has ever happened before. The same Jesus of Nazareth who enthralled us with miracles and healings, who inspired us with his teaching and his promise of the kingdom, who carried us along in his challenge to the oppressive powers of his day, this same Jesus who was tortured and killed now stands in our midst—resplendent and transfigured beyond anything we could imagine.

He eats with us. He drinks with us. He soothes our fears by the power of his presence and he bids us peace. As we receive his Spirit we can feel his breath warm on our faces—we know ourselves to be forever one-ed with him. The energy of his risen body flows into our bodies so that we know him in our own bodily self-presence.

If Jesus of Nazareth has indeed been raised from the dead, and if he is present to us in this way, then nothing matters now except to be with him. Blessed Julian says this a little differently when she tells us that the greatest wisdom we can have in this life is for us to "bind ourselves with Him and fix ourselves intimately to Him ever more, in whatever state we are" (*Lesson*, Chapter 76).

For those on the contemplative way, being with Jesus, remaining with him in his risen presence, occurs through a paradoxical journey into our own deepest reality, into hiddenness. Answering the question of the bride who asks of the divine Bridegroom, "Where have you hidden?" John of the Cross answered,

> Oh then, soul, most beautiful among all creatures, so anxious to know the dwelling place of your Beloved so you may go in search of him and be united with him, now we are telling you that you yourself are his dwelling and his secret inner room and hiding place. There is reason for you to be elated and joyful in seeing that all your good and hope is so close as to be within you, or better, that you cannot be without him. . . . What more do you want, O soul! And what else do you search for outside, when within yourself you possess your riches, delights, satisfaction, fullness, and kingdom—your Beloved whom you desire and seek? Be joyful and gladdened in your interior recollection with him, for you have him so close to you. Desire him there, adore him there. Do not go in pursuit of him outside yourself. (*Spiritual Canticle*, 1.7–8)

There is no need to go in pursuit of the risen Lord outside ourselves. We will not find him as long as we are looking for some especially holy thing or experience. As John of the Cross says, we will only become distracted and wearied by outward searching. When we let go of the obsessive search outside ourselves for something to make us happy, when we relax and move fully into the present moment, then we know, however inchoately, that we already possess all that we desire within ourselves. His risen Life is within us. The glory and the joy of his risen body pass into the felt experience of our own bodies. The work of contemplative love, knowing that nothing matters now except to be with him, the risen Lord, is just this work of surrendering and being present exactly where we are, knowing and loving him in our own bodies, in the very center of our being. Our most fundamental feeling of being here is a feeling of being with him and in him.

No Going Back to Normal

D URING HOLY WEEK THE ORDINARY LIFE of the monastery is set aside. Almost all of our energy and time is devoted to the Holy Week liturgies and preparations for the Easter festivities. Our chapel itself, the very center of our lives, is emptied of all signs of holiness at the end of Holy Week.

This happens mostly on the evening of Maundy Thursday, following the foot-washing and Eucharist in our refectory and the dinner of roasted lamb and "bitter herbs." We then proceed to the chapel for the stripping of the altar. First, the Blessed Sacrament is removed from the tabernacle and placed in a side altar. The fair linen and frontal are taken off the altar, revealing a bare altar stone. Candlestands and the silver Gospel book are removed along with any other precious item. Lights are extinguished and the gates that define the chapel as a holy place are swung wide open. It is as if the crowd of authorities and soldiers who had arrested Jesus had swept through our chapel as well, leaving it empty and desolate. There is a real sense of the sacredness having been violated and forcibly taken away. The chapel then remains in this state through Good Friday and Holy Saturday, until the Great Vigil of Easter when the altar vestments, candles, lights, silver trimmings, and the Blessed Sacrament are restored along with a lavish display of lilies and fresh flowers.

With the chapel restored to its more usual state and the rhythm of ordinary life picking up again on Easter Monday, it is understandable to feel some relief, to catch oneself thinking, "Thank God we are back to normal!"

But if Easter and the incredible proclamation of Jesus' resurrection means anything, it is that there is no going back to normal ever again. What we call "normal" died with Jesus on the cross. As we step back into seemingly normal life again after the drama of Holy Week and Easter, we are standing on the cusp of the unknown, the possibility of a totally new and different way of life. Hardly able to stand, we grasp about for support, blinking in the blinding light of a new and risen life that is now being offered us to live in the resplendent body of Jesus.

But what exactly is this new life? What does it mean to live the risen life of Christ now? To enter eternal life already?

The meaning of the Resurrection is notoriously difficult to get a handle on. Although we can talk about death and sin being overcome as St. Paul does, and although we can throw ourselves with gusto into the Easter celebrations, the actual reality of resurrection for most of us still seems too distant and too strange to have an immediate bearing on our lives. In the monastery I have experienced several Easter seasons during which I did not know what to make of the celebration. I knew that I was supposed to be joyful, but I could not have told you why. Jesus was raised and, yes, I could trace out some intellectual application of this in theology, but what did it mean for my life now? Many people have this same difficulty in connecting with the power of the Resurrection.

There is an old saying, used to encourage meditation on Scripture: stay with the word until the Word breaks through.

This encapsulates the Christian experience of faithfully attending on the all-too-human words of Scripture, reflecting and entering imaginatively into them, until we find ourselves in the presence of God himself. Our meditation ceases to be our rumination on a text and becomes an encounter with a living person who steps into our lives with his own autonomous authority, who makes demands on us, who calls us into love.

If we are ever to taste the reality of the Resurrection for ourselves, knowing its force in our lives now, we have to begin with this kind of faithful attention to Scriptures, ruminating on them, chewing over them slowly and thoughtfully, opening our imaginations and our emotional life to the images, stories, and ideas contained in them. For Christians seeking to know Christ, this is a daily habit—not something we do when we feel like it. It is a daily commitment to go to Scripture and, even when it is a barren exercise, to stay with the word of God out of sheer devotion, until God himself does in fact break through.

Our contemplative practices of silent meditation and mindfullness throughout the day (see the breathing exercises at the end of this book) provide a rich context for our meditation on the Word of God. In our contemplative stillness and silence, we have learned how to step aside, at least momentarily, from the chattering of our anxious egoic selves. We practice letting this self go as a distraction. Over the course of months and years of faithful practice, this creates a silence and a depth in ourselves in which we can receive God's word into the core of our being, allowing God to utter his words in the very center of our hearts. Then the Word himself can indeed break through with life-changing authority and power. And we begin to know our lives not as a desperate effort to somehow get things right, but as a response to a living presence who has stepped in and who seeks through us, here and now, to begin making all things new. To be fair, it took about fifteen years of monastic life for me to begin to get a sense of the living meaning of the Resurrection, and since then the Resurrection has become the integrating center for all my spiritual life, practice, and commitment. This reality is something that I can't fully communicate. Each person has to discover for himself through his own faithfulness, staying with the word until the Word himself breaks through. Nobody can do this for anyone else. We all have to take on the loving work of silence and meditation.

What I can say is this: alienation, sin, and death are indeed overcome in the Resurrected Christ. When we experience him stepping as a living reality into our lives, we know ourselves as recepients of a tremendous love, a love not only for us as "souls," but a love even for our bodies, a cherishing and celebrating of the history of our embodied lives. We find ourselves living in a world where the horizon of life is not the darkness of death, but the effulgence and fullness of life, given now, in a felt and experiential way, into our own bodies. We discover the possibility of peace rather than anxiety and presence rather than isolation. The love of God becomes something known in our bodies rather than just as a thought in our heads. It becomes a felt reality.

A friend recently asked me if I have had an experience of God. I didn't know what to say. There was a time when I thought it possible to have a discrete experience of God that could be separated from the rest of life. But now I'm not sure this is even possible or desirable. What I experience is simply myself as an embodied creature, and the more mindful and present I am in myself as a physical body here and now, the more this is simply felt as a state of connection, openness, presence. I call this "eternal life" because it does not have much to do with the ego's anxious trek through time. I also call it "knowing Jesus," and receiving his resurrection into myself. But it's not a discrete experience I can point to. It is a felt dimension of fully being in my body, in the present moment, here and now, regardless of what I am experiencing. Everything else is simply mental distraction.

The Heat Is Off

THE HUMAN SPECIES IS NOT MORE GREEDY FOR LIFE than are other species—every living thing fights tooth and nail for its own advancement. To give up possibilities for ourselves seems to run counter to our very genetic coding. And yet we know also, just as deeply in ourselves, that we were not put here for ourselves, but to serve God, to give glory to Another whose creation this is. Our species exists not primarily for its own advancement but as servants to creation as a whole. The promise of resurrection affects this, even makes it possible, because it offers total human fulfillment partially independent of history.

Without the Resurrection, we have two choices: we can be either this-worldly or other-worldly. Either we throw ourselves into this-worldly greed, or we engage in an other-worldly spirituality of violence against this world and our bodies. Either way we find ourselves denying the goodness of life on earth. Either way we are acting in violence and in self-seeking. But there is a third path, a path that is not simply greed softened by religious or ethical concerns. Our hearts, after all, are made to yearn desperately and deeply for a fullness of existence—this is the drive behind all life. Are we really locked into a situation where we either indulge this drive or have to cut violently against it, hoping it eventually goes away?

With the Resurrection, we discover a third path, neither this-worldly nor other-worldly, but that of the kingdom of God. The Resurrection suggests that our deepest human longings are fulfilled in our being taken up into the risen body of Jesus, our mortal bodies not being stripped off, as St. Paul says, but taken up into the immortal. Once we taste this and know this fulfillment in ourselves, we can leave the tragic competition for more life that is destroying the earth without slipping into the opposite of being spiritually violent against ourselves.

When we already know our fulfillment coming to us in the gift of the Resurrected One, we experience relief and release from the terrible pressure to get everything for ourselves in this life. That terrible pressure to get, to go, to be, to achieve, to access new experiences is removed. Stepping into the reality of resurrection, we step out of a scarcity of life into an abundance in Christ, in his gift of himself. We step out of anxiety into peace. The very sense we have of our embodied existence is changed from that of being constantly under threat, to that of being opened to an endless new life that is simply given to us, lavished on us in the apparent nothingness of contemplative silence and presence. Moreover, this newfound sense of abundance and inner peace, and the inner strength and stability these create, allow us to give our lives away for others.

The Resurrection is what enabled the apostles, who had originally abandoned Jesus in his suffering, to walk with such calm into martyrdom. It is what brings compassion, gentleness, and kindness to birth in us—not as nice virtues that we force down on our greedy and combative selves, but qualities of resurrected existence that emerge from within like a blooming flower. We walk with Christ's life on this earth and we live to serve God by serving humanity and the life of the planet as a whole.

Eros and Embodied Joy

IN HIS MEDITATIONS ON THE RESURRECTION, St. Paul says that "in this tent we groan, under our burden, because we wish not to be unclothed but to be further clothed, so that what is mortal may be swallowed up by life. He who has prepared us for this very thing is God, who has given us the Spirit as a guarantee" (2 Corinthians 5:4–5).

For years this language of putting the immortal on over the mortal has puzzled me, because it made the immortal body seem so extrinsic—like a new set of clothes. Was Paul simply running out of effective metaphors and falling back on the clumsy example of clothing? I don't think so. I have come to find in this passage a dazzlingly clear expression of the body's most fundamental longing, a longing not to be destroyed (stripped off) but to be drawn up into and transfused with the brilliance of God's own life. I think this bodily yearning is the root of all desire, the eros that is the fundamental energy of the universe. I don't want to embarrass anyone, but we do have this physical desire in our bodies to be taken up, held, enclosed, and transfused with an Other's desire. Our bodies yearn to be enfolded and permeated by that Other's Life and Light. The resurrection of Jesus Christ is God's fulfillment of this desire, first in Jesus' body, and secondly for all of us in our bodies. Easter leads then to a reappraisal of the nuptial mysticism we find in St. Bernard and in many of the late medieval women mystics. I find in Easter an invitation to relate to God and the risen body of Jesus from the center of my own body's longing.

When we practice the contemplative life of daily silent prayer, conscientious mindfulness, and inner awareness, we are engaged in beautiful disciplines that prepare us in our bodies to receive the full gift of resurrection for which we yearn. But the way is not always straightforward; in order for our bodies to be opened to God's life, we often have to become aware of desires that we have spent our whole lives trampling down. Our contemplative practice will bring into our awareness the disordered desires that fill our bodily life. Instead of briefly fulfilling these desires in semiconscious activity or simply repressing them, the discipline of the contemplative way forces us to become fully cognizant of them. We actually come to know the yearning in our bodies for the divine life. The wondrous thing is that, once we are aware of this, we can use this energy in prayer, where we find our whole being reaching up in great physical and spiritual power for the gift of God's life to us. Yearning itself, when consciously felt and accepted, is purifying and cleansing in its pain—think of St. Paul's groans—and prepares us for the gift of embodied joy and life and light that God wants to give.

Absence Is for Growth

A T SOME POINT IN YOUR LIFE, you will lose someone who took care of you, who helped you to feel that you were OK. The loss or death of such people, often your parents themselves, can leave you feeling unsure of yourself and perhaps not ready to take up the mantle of responsibility that they have left behind.

Yet their absence is also an invitation to grow up into greater strength and maturity. We can't depend on someone else to do this. At some point in all of our lives, we will each have this charge and this responsibility.

The parallel to Christ's ascension is obvious. What would have happened if Christ had stayed forever, appearing at breakfast and giving advice about that day's fishing? All problems could have been solved, and all questions answered by directing everything to him. But Christian faith and the contemplative way are not an escape from responsibility, allowing someone else, obviously divinized, to bear the burden so that one can enjoy dependency. We all have to step up and carry the mystery of God's love for the next generation.

In the contemplative way, this experience of hard loss inviting growth and greater maturity is a well-known spiritual dynamic. After being nurtured for years on consolations of intellectual certainty or meaningfulness in life, these apparent graces are withdrawn. There is a loss of certainty and a sense only of absence and loss where God used to be. In a striking image from John of the Cross, God smears the divine breast with bitter herbs so that, weaned off the consolations that were keeping us infantile, we mature in our relationship with God and begin to live on solid food. There is a point in which we have to choose faith, or choose to live as though we knew or experienced faith as something real. While this seems like walking in darkness, the saints who have gone before us tell us that this is the only way we will grow up. The God whom we have known has to die so that we can discover more of God's reality and grow up out of dependencies. We learn what it means to walk in faith and learn, slowly, to appreciate the almost inchoate knowledge that is given, the new solidification and strengthening of ourselves in the mission to be God's presence in the world.

If this is intimidating, we can take comfort in the promised gift of the Holy Spirit, which is our only hope for such a task. This is the gift we wait for in the nine still and hopeful days between Ascension and Pentecost. The Jesus we knew is gone; we are awaiting the power that will enable us to make Jesus present to the world through us.

In Humility Awaiting the Gift of the Holy Spirit

I N THE CHURCH'S TRADITION THERE IS a nine-day period between the Ascension of Christ into heaven and the descent of the Holy Spirit. These nine days were the origin of the devotional practice of the novena—nine days of prayer offered before significant events or for special concerns.

It is striking that in the Lukan accounts of this nine-day interlude the believers are instructed by our Lord to wait in Jerusalem—not to go out and make disciples, or preach, or set up shop as rabbis of the New Way, but simply to wait. This waiting without direction or certainty prepared them for the gift of the Holy Spirit. They would be emptied by nine days of waiting so that they could receive the inflow of a life different than their own. The presence of their Resurrected Lord—such a triumph and such a comfort to the apostles—was taken away and all they could do, in obedience to the dominical command, was to wait for they-knew-not-what, a promised gift from God.

This resonates with what we experience in our own lives. We often have to traverse long periods of emptiness and apparent futility when all that we experienced of God is drained from our lives before we are ready or willing to receive the gift of a totally new way of life. Sometimes we interfere with this process by frantically running around doing all sorts of good things, trying to recapture the zeal or certainty we once knew. Instead of allowing the apparent absence of God to ring through the depths of our being, we obscure our loss by fabricating a grace-less godliness.

In the collects and readings for this time of the liturgical year, we are continually advised that as baptized Christians, our lives are hidden with Christ in God and we should allow our hearts and minds to be drawn by Christ up to heaven and "there with him to continually dwell." This is what our waiting is to consist of—a kind of open ascension of our consciousness with Christ into heavenly reality.

This is hard to understand, and we naturally chafe at the suggestion that we should "ascend" out of this earth, at least mentally, to dwell in heaven with Christ. This suggests the kind of angelic spirituality, with its renunciation of the physical earth and the physical body and an exaltation of mental states and the cerebral control of the self, that we are rightly suspicious of. Is this kind of hyper-spiritualism really what this time is about? Is this what it means to wait in the absence of our Lord for the gift of the Spirit?

St. Benedict in his Rule suggests a completely different way. Ascending into heaven—and for that matter, faithful waiting— is not accomplished by a kind of spiritual violence against ourselves, launching our minds up into a preoccupation with heavenly things. No, for St. Benedict, the way we ascend into heavenly reality is by the practice of humility. In chapter seven of his Rule, Benedict gives us a picture of the humble brother as one who is willing to wait because he does not regard his work or words or plans to be most important or edifying. Such a brother also practices a free and flowing obedience and a glad penance.

This idea of the descent of humility as being actually an ascent to God is applicable to any life anywhere. It is not reserved as a monastic virtue but is a Christian virtue, modeled on

Christ's own life. What the saints tell us is that God is with us each moment of the day, that heaven is right now all about us and within us. Moreover, what prevents us from living in this divine presence is largely our anxious self-concern, driving us out of the present moment into mental distractions and the unconsciousness of all-consuming moods.

Humility is, in essence, the practice of first being willing to be present in our own skin and our own life, where we actually are. It means letting go of the fantasy life in our heads in order to be present to what is happening in our bodies and around us in this moment. This in turn allows us to be aware when we are beginning to slip off into anxious self-concern or moodiness, defensiveness, aggressiveness, or distraction. These are all different manifestations of the ego exalting itself and being centered on itself. We can feel the tension in our bodies when this happens, or the mental sickness in a whir of obsessive thoughts. Doing away with these things, we can then practice letting go of the anxious urge to dominate a conversation, or to push through a crowded store, or to talk about ourselves, or to vent a mood. Letting go of these things can feel like a little death. But in practicing humility in everyday life like this, we discover a kind of peaceful return to our natural simplicity and presence. We discover we can indeed stand in the presence of God here and now, that we ascend into heaven to be with Christ by this kind of humble action. Moreover, we experience this not as a kind of boundaryless place where we let others abuse us, but as a place where we rediscover and step into our own dignity as persons and find a real strength within us to say "no" to abuse or injustice.

◠Loving God's Presence◠
in the Different, the Strange, the Other

I F I WERE ASKED WHAT "being filled with the Holy Spirit" means for a contemplative, I would not know what to say. Would he be struck by new compunction? Or great insights? Would she be drawn into hours of prayer when she is hidden even from herself? Would he be filled with joyful charity, a radical selflessness that spreads light and life wherever he goes? Or would she gain a new reticence and repose that makes her appear less charitable than usual? The answer, I would guess, is yes to all these questions. At different times and in different ways the Spirit works differently in each of us. The fruits of the Holy Spirit—love, joy, peace, patience, kindness, goodness, fidelity, gentleness, and self-control—are each manifested in diverse ways in each of us, sometimes so diverse as to seem contradictory!

When we pray at Pentecost, then, for the gift of the Holy Spirit, there's no clear direction ahead of time on what we are praying for, only for authentic openness to the gift of God's Spirit and our responsive obedience to the Spirit's promptings.

Yet there is one feast, a feast that often falls near Pentecost, that speaks with special meaning to the contemplative heart. This is the feast of the Visitation of the Blessed Virgin Mary to St. Elizabeth, an event recorded in the first chapter of Luke's Gospel. This story is exploding with the Holy Spirit. The Blessed Virgin Mary, having just chosen to give herself to God's will that she might bear Jesus by the power of the Spirit, "hurries off" to her much older relative, Elizabeth, who herself is pregnant with John the Baptist. As Mary comes through her door, John the Baptist leaps in Elizabeth's womb, she is filled with God's Spirit, and she exclaims, "God's blessing is on you above all women, and his blessing is on the fruit of your womb!" Then Mary, in response to Elizabeth's words and praise, herself is lifted by the Holy Spirit to offer her Magnificat, "My soul magnifies the Lord, and my spirit rejoices in God my Savior" (Luke 1:46–47).

A sure sign of the Holy Spirit's presence is that we are able to recognize God's presence in others, in those who are different from us. It's not so much that we ouselves perceive, think, and come to the considered conclusion that God's presence just might be in the person across from us. Rather, the life of God that is in us suddenly and surprisingly leaps up for joy at the proximity of someone else who is also bearing that same life within him. This presence may be entirely hidden from the external world. It may be hardly conceived.

But if we are gifted with the Holy Spirit, we can be struck deep within ourselves by a recognition of God in others. This is, in effect, the recognition of our own deepest self in another, and is most especially a gift and most especially disturbing when the other in whom we know God to be is very different from us, perhaps of a different religion or not religious at all. The Spirit in us sees and knows others in a way deeper than whatever our little intellect with its miserly judgments can muster. It leaps, and we respond.

When we begin our walk in intimacy with God, this awareness of the divine life in others, a felt resonance between our and their deepest reality, will likely happen only with people we already trust and love or look up to. We may meet a particularly holy person and have this experience for the first time. We may look into the eyes of our partner, our spouse, and suddenly know we share the same depth. But as we grow spiritually this felt experience of underlying resonance and union extends to less intimate friends, to lesser acquaintances, and then even to strangers. No longer living on the surface of life, but living with our sense of God engaged, we are able to sense God in others. Further along on the way, we can have this same experience with people whom we might consider our rivals or enemies, or with people who, on the surface of life, are frightening or unpleasant. This experience is something we cannot engineer. It is something that is given and grows according to its own potential. Our job is to remain open to it, and we nurture it by fidelity to prayer and silence and spiritual practice.

Whatever the graces and gifts that God may lavish upon us at Pentecost, whatever being filled with the Holy Spirit might mean for us at this point in our lives, one thing remains consistent: an authentic presence of God's life within us will always awaken us to God's life in others, in a circle of inclusion that is continuously growing wider. We find a union with our most distant and different brothers and sisters, based on nothing else than a recognition that, under the myriad distinctions of outward life, this other person, so different and perhaps so alien to me, is already living the same Life as I am, the life of God.

⟶ ORDINARY TIME

ORDINARY TIME IS ONE OF THE NAMES GIVEN for the season following Pentecost and running until the beginning of the next liturgical year in Advent. We thus spend just about half the year in Ordinary Time, and after the extraordinary seasons of Lent, Holy Week, and Easter, entering this less dramatic season often feels like a blessed release and relief. During Ordinary Time our task is to take the one or two things we have learned in our experience of the Paschal Mystery and to knead it like leaven through dough into the rest of our lives.

In the monastery where I live, Ordinary Time includes the last part of spring, all of summer, all of autumn, and the beginning of winter. It is marked by the great feasts of Corpus Christi in June, Sts. Peter and Paul in July, St. Mary the Virgin in August, Holy Cross Day in September, and All Saints and All Souls days in early November, with a great many lesser feasts scattered along the way. The daily and weekly schedules run their usual and blessedly ordinary course. Every day except for Sundays we are up for 5:00 Morning Prayer, followed by silence until Eucharist at 7:00. Then there is breakfast and then work until noonday prayer, dinner, and siesta. The afternoons are a combination of community time and work until Evensong at 5:00, followed by supper, free time, then silent meditation and Compline, ending at a quarter past eight. This daily schedule, called our *horarium*, is like a great, rythmic heartbeat that keeps life flowing through the whole body of the monastic community.

Each meditation in this section is an exploration of what it means to live more deeply into a contemplative vocation in the midst of the ordinariness of life, carrying the incomparable gift of our Christian faith into everyday life and finding there the presence of the Holy.

Unceasing Response to Love

THE GOAL OF THE CONTEMPLATIVE LIFE IS SUMMED UP in St. Paul's exhortation to pray without ceasing. In the Middle Ages, this led to a monastic culture in which it was assumed that the more time you spent in church chanting psalms the better. Some communities even tried to institute a twenty-four-hour round of choral prayer so that what the individual could not accomplish the community could. But these efforts are aberrations, and they are based on a misunderstanding of prayer.

The Book of Common Prayer defines prayer as "responding to God, by thought and by deeds, with or without words." With this definition, unceasing prayer is wonderfully revealed as a state of unceasing responsiveness to God. Here we begin to glimpse a state of life that is possible for us, profound and beautiful. We realize too that in order for the whole energy and movement of our life to be a supple, joyful, immediate responsiveness to God, our hearts and minds need to be purified of all the selfishness, anxiety, drama—all the antagonism that makes us blind and deaf to God and unable to respond to the movement of God's desire.

In a well-ordered monastery, unceasing prayer is understood as unceasing response to God in the delight of love, as much in the garden and the kitchen as when one is in choir or sitting in meditation. No particular aspect of life—work, the daily office, meditation, silence, contemplation—is given absolute priority, since all are different ways of responding to God's love.

Understood correctly, washing the dishes can be as much the goal of monastic existence as contemplation. It is natural for a person new to monastic life to imagine that she is going to spend huge swaths of time in prayer. And we do pray in the formal sense for about four hours a day. But we also turn compost, clean the roadside ditch, run spreadsheets, and troubleshoot problems with our Web server. It is great when a novice Sister is able to put her heart as much into these assignments as into formal prayer.

Traditionally, the key tool used by monastic legislators to purify the heart and to encourage monks and nuns to practice unceasing response to God was the horarium, the daily schedule. Precisely because there are specified times for prayer, for work, for study, for talking, for silence, an overall communal culture could be established and maintained, and individual monks and nuns could feel that in living this life they were being taken up into a rhythm, a breathing, a flowing in and out of God that transcended their individual fancies. No aspect is defined as being a time without prayer, a time where one stops responding to God. Thus there is in the end no good reason to resist the horarium, since the final goal of one's whole life—responding in love to God—can be realized everywhere.

What this means is that the monk or nun, in being called by the ringing of the bell to put down one activity and proceed to another, is bound to discover his or her inner attachments to one activity over another. The experience of frustration, anxiety, anger, petulance, greed—any kind of inner turbulence—in being asked to live in the horarium reveals where the monk's heart is not really set on unceasing response to God, but has rather become inflamed with an ego-based fascination with some other goal or satisfaction. In recognizing the inner turbulence caused by the unending round of bells, and taking responsibility for that turbulence by stepping beyond it, the monk undergoes a painful purification of his own motives. His heart is slowly freed of self-love and indulgent gratifications.

But contemplatives do not have to live in monasteries to experience this purification. A person advancing on the contemplative way will likely draw up for herself a rule of life to which she holds herself accountable, usually with the help of a Spiritual Director. The inner chafing at not being able to keep watching a movie because one has to fulfill an obligation to contemplative prayer, or because one has to leave meditation to engage in one's work—any form of inner turbulence reveals the presence of self-will, and thus a partial inability to live in unceasing response to God. Having a spiritual community, in which a common rule of life is followed and in which the experience of failure in keeping the rule or turbulence in keeping it, is invaluable.

Such work of purification is not, however, limited to the daily and weekly reflections on one's experience of keeping a rule of life. When a traffic signal causes anger, when a colleague acts in a way that brings rage to the heart, when one is possessed by an obsessive desire for something, when one is anxious and dramatic in a relationship—in all these very common experiences, the soul has ceased to be open to God. Both body and soul are turbulent, becoming defensive or aggressive. The advancing contemplative recognizes the situations that cause such experiences as graciously given by God to help him to know himself. Instead of blaming traffic signals and colleagues for his distress, he steps into a clear awareness of his selfish, hard, embittered spirit, and then steps beyond it by surrendering pain and ego-based anxiety to God time and time again, a thousand times a day.

As we proceed and practice with others, we learn helpful ways of letting go of turbulence in our body and spirit and returning peacefully to the place of open, dynamic, creative response in the midst of work as well as prayer. We discover that it is basically a question of inner freedom, and the possibility of authentic joy.

Love of the Puppets

I N A REMARKABLE POEM CALLED "Love of the Puppets"[6] Richard Wilbur describes a journey from selfish desire through despair to tender intimacy and communion. When the puppets who give the poem its title first seek communion, they do so in a spirit of lust and desire:

> April, unready to be so intense,
> Marked time while these outstripped the gentle weather,
> Yielded their natures to insensate sense,
> And flew apart the more they came together.

> Where did they fly? Why each through such a storm
> As may be conjured in a globe of glass
> Drive on the colder as the flesh grew warm
> In breathless haste to be at lust's impasse.

This leads to a kind of marriage, a desire to control the partner, exhaustion and disillusionment:

> To cross the little bridge and sink to rest
> In visions of the snow-occluded house
> Where languishes, unfounded by any quest,
> The perfect, small, asphyxiated spouse.

> The blizzard ended, and their eyes grew clear,
> And there they lay exhausted yet unsated;
> Why did their features run with tear on tear,
> Until their looks were individuated?

What is so inspiring is that the puppets discover that through their very sense of lack and loneliness they are able to be present to each other in a new and total way. In accepting themselves and the other, they enter the long-sought-for intimacy and communion with each other:

> One peace implies another, and they cried
> For want of love as if their souls would crack
> Till, in despair of being satisfied,
> They vowed at least to share each other's lack.
>
> Then maladroitly they embraced once more,
> And hollow rang to hollow with a sound
> That turned the brooks more sweetly than before,
> And made the birds explode for miles around.

I am almost certain that Wilbur wrote this poem out of his experience of marriage, but it speaks eloquently of the journey to intimacy with God in the contemplative life. When we begin the spiritual life, we often are "loving God for our own sake" (to quote Bernard of Clairvaux). We are seeking God for ourselves. We are filled with spiritual desires. This leads in time to some kind of spiritual and religious commitment, but as anyone who has walked this path will tell you, it is only after one has made a commitment that the bottom often seems to drop out. Satisfaction in God seems infinitely far away. We may experience nothing but absence. Instead of a Divine Love to ravish us into union, we discover the "perfect, small, asphyxiated" idol that we have made for ourselves.

Many people lose heart at this point, or simply forget their original desires and try to content themselves with being only half-satisfied. It seems, after all, that religion has let us down, and spirituality is getting us nowhere. The God we once desired so fervently, and to whom we may be publicly committed, does not even seem to exist. Wondering what happened, we are tempted to become a little resentful or even cynical about religious practice.

But instead of dropping out or contenting oneself with being half-satisfed, or growing resentful and cynical, there is another way: we bravely step through our experience of lack and choose to remain committed, choose to keep searching, choose to look for a deeper understanding of God in our relationship with him. To return to the metaphor of marriage, we make a choice to step beyond ourselves, and we seek to understand, know, and love our partner more deeply, helping them to come alive. Our love and desire is directed by our conscious choice to help them to flourish.

In Christianity, Jesus in his life, his ministry, his death and resurrection is the definitive presence of God to us, God's speaking, God's self-disclosure. Having run into what looks like a dead end in our spiritual life, we make the conscious decision not to abandon this word of God, but to seek to know him, his concerns, his desire, and even his suffering more deeply. We step beyond ourselves and seek to know God more fully in Christ. It is this choice, made over and over again as we proceed through all the changes of life, that gives us access to new intimacy with God, in which, no longer seeing ourselves quite so much, we take on God's own concerns and God's loving. Knowing God and giving ourselves to him in this way, however "maladroitly," we just might hear the "birds explode for miles around."

Shooting the Rapids of Change

THERE ARE TIMES IN LIFE WHEN our external situation becomes quite stable. What we face each day and what gifts we might enjoy are predictable. It is often at times such as these—if we don't fall into boredom—when we are able to accomplish great things in our lives. We move deeply into prayer. We create expressions of our lives that we can pass on to others. We are able to taste the mystery of life in stillness and peace.

Yet life, as we all know, never stays the same for too long. Often the placid river comes just before the white-water rapids and the waterfall. We are called unexpectedly into greater responsibility, a greater extension of our selves, into new flexibility and new life. Yet even in times of change, when we are confronted with new questions and difficulties, it is salutary to remember how through all of this the core issue of our vocation—our desire for God and God's desire for us—has not changed. Even if it is obscured in the daily confusion, that core vocation is still there.

Someone once said that mediocre philosophers jump from question to question throughout the course of their lives, but great minds find themselves dealing over and over with one question that enthralls them and defines the meaning of their whole life's work. Most of us are not philosophers, but in following the contemplative way we are responding to a core summons to love God in all things, through all things, and for all things.

We can, however, become distracted from this, allowing ourselves to be pushed around from question to question, one spiritual school to another, spiritual experience to spiritual hope, reacting to each stimulus that passes by. The danger is that we skitter about on the surface of life and never move into the depths. It takes courage to respond wholeheartedly to the single overmastering concern that is the heart of our personality, instead of dithering out our lives in endless little issues, experiments, and improvisations. Especially during times of change and outward commotion, it is essential to make times of quiet where we can let go of the fuss and distraction and make contact with the core questions and issues at the heart of our lives. Then we discover that even amid commotion and change the center still remains within us, even if it is only the peace of the still and waiting question.

Journaling Around the Secret

KEEPING A JOURNAL IS HELPFUL TO MANY PEOPLE seeking to grow in love and a purpose in a life centered in God. I have kept journals on and off ever since I was a teenager and an aspiring writer. It is, however, almost always embarrassing to read my old journals, to listen to the urgent or fascinated voices that fill them. I read over the record of my thoughts, feelings, and intuitions, and in hindsight they all seem somewhat unreal. None of them, it seems, actually touch on the work of grace.

But occasionally I will come across a passage completely devoid of me and my self-proccupation, when I had written about the sound of rain on the flashing, or the color of a sparrow's feathers, or the smells in the air just after a shower. Suddenly, the words seem vibrant, alive, shimmering.

Our spiritual growth is almost never what we think or feel it is, and is recognizable only in hindsight. In hindsight, we can indeed spot the working of grace, a mysterious evolution happening far underneath the buzz and whirl of our conscious selves, and yet bringing us to the place and person and relative wholeness that we now find ourselves to have. On an outward level, the urgencies and fascinations recorded in my journals spin themselves on and on, but grace is working with me on a much deeper level.

Does this mean that I should stop writing, stop keeping my journal? I don't think so. It is amazingly helpful for us to spend even just ten minutes a day jotting down what we are experiencing, thinking, hoping for. It helps us to live more consciously. Charles Williams once wrote that we have to build altars to God precisely so that God's lightning can strike somewhere else. Likewise, we have to do what we can to process our experience and define our reality in terms of our thinking and feeling and intuiting, recognizing that the mystery of grace will most likely happen elsewhere, on an altar other than the one we imagined for ourselves.

No Time for
Itsy-Bitsy Statues

FOR THOSE SEEKING TO DEEPEN THEIR LIVES OF PRAYER and contemplative practice, belonging to a religious community is all but essential. It's doubtful whether any of us could advance beyond spiritual self-seeking without the supporting structure of an external community and the bracing challenges that it offers to us.

If we go it alone, we are liable to encounter nothing but ourselves. This leads to spiritual tedium—to being stuck in a place where everything remains in our own control. We are then unable to trust ourselves to the movement of a community's life in faith. The rituals, beliefs, wisdom, and spiritual traditions of a community guide, challenge, and inform us as we seek a deeper life.

At the same time, it's crucial to see that this same religious structure can be used very powerfully to give us the semblance of living deeply and religiously while in fact we go on skimming the surface of our own existence, propelled like a water strider on a pond, constantly skittering about in fear or desire, distraction or anxiety. We may think, for instance, that because we are saying holy words, making profound comments, that we are actually living the depths of holiness. This is not necessarily so. In my experience there is a great chasm between thought and words and actual life, and one has to be very vigilant not to fool oneself. And what goes for words goes for the rest of the religious stuff in our lives as well, be it rituals or icons or prayer-ropes or even a contemplative prayer practice. Taking on external demands and practices is indeed essential, but it is only the first step, and to use it as a cloak for a lack of conversion to living in the depths is a constant danger.

I am reminded of an often-quoted passage from Thomas Merton: "There is always a temptation to diddle around in the contemplative life, making itsy-bitsy statues." Annie Dillard, quoting Merton, adds: "There is always an enormous temptation in all of life to diddle around making itsy-bitsy friends and meals and journeys for itsy-bitsy years on end."[7]

We do well to periodically ask ourselves if we're living as deeply as our religious words and practices seem to imply, or if we are merely using them to make ourselves feel occasionally better. Are we giving too much license to the old self, with its desire to skitter on the surface of existence, never stopping?

The traditional vows of religious orders can be helpful in structuring this kind of critical reflection. *Chastity* asks us about our relationships with other people: Are we using other people for our own sake? Are we able to stand in the presence of another as one who bears in herself the whole mystery of redemption? Are we growing in our awareness of a depth of inviolate innocence in ourselves that belongs wholly to God?

Poverty points to our relationship to material things: Are we using a preoccupation with things and money in order to avoid the emptiness of our own hearts, or the deeper demands of this life? Have we lost ourselves in the pursuit of material security?

Obedience points to our relationship with our own wills, desires, preferences, and opinions. How much are we living on a two-dimensional surface, propelled easily about by our desires and preferences? How much have we allowed obedience, holy listening, and quick response to cut across this two-dimensional skittering and force us into the depths where we encounter our own craving?

Finally, the vow of *prayer and conversion of life* asks us if we might not be filling our minds and hearts with itsy-bitsy stuff, perpetual distractions, instead of engaging something deeper.

The Desert Fathers tell of a young monk who visits his Abba and shares with him the good news that he is not experiencing any temptations or passions. The good Abba tells him, however, that this is only because he is not making any effort. In my terms, he is skating along the surface, and the whole of his religious life is just a pleasing novelty. The Abba tells him that he is like a house with all his windows and doors open; the wind of the passions is indeed blowing through the house, but because none of it is restrained, the young monk does not feel it. He advises the young monk to start closing some doors and windows so he will experience the groaning of the house as the winds are caught inside.

When we stop spinning new religious stuff constantly around ourselves, but engage with our tradition with a persistent commitment, we start closing the doors and windows and begin to find out who we really are.

Listening for God
Through our Bodies

S T. BENEDICT'S RULE BEGINS WITH the command to "listen!" In order to listen well, we have to be comfortable in ourselves, still in our bodies, and directed outward toward the other person in an eagerness for their good. This is why the statue of St. Benedict outside the cathedral in Norwich, England, has his finger pressed to his lips in the gesture of silence. We can't listen to God until we are calm in ourselves, quiet in our thoughts, and eager in love to know and respond to God more fully. St. Benedict envisioned his monks living largely in silence, not merely to keep them from getting in each other's hair, or as some esoteric spiritual practice, or as punishment, but out of humility. They were also to be silent in a desire to listen to God's speaking on so many different levels, a divine speaking that simply cannot be heard if we are always chattering.

Each one of us can look at our lives and find places and times where it would be especially helpful to be silent. For many, the mornings provide the best time for the practice of silence, before others have woken up, before our days have begun. Such a practice of outward silence can begin with not turning on the radio or the television the moment we wake up. It can continue into monitoring the interior noise that we sometimes create in our heads as we shower and dress, without even thinking about it. This interior radio has to be turned off as well. Do you know that it has an off button—that you can shower and dress without a constant monologue (or dialogue) of worries and desires being broadcast by your false self in your head? It does have an off switch!

We learn silence best by learning how to be present in our bodies—and when we are showering and dressing this is a wonderful, relaxing, and pleasurable time to pay attention to what we are feeling. It is a way of caring for our physical selves, being fully present to our bodily reality. The breathing exercises known in almost every spiritual tradition are of great help— following our in and out breaths with little prayers. This is a powerful way to let go of the anxious need for constant inner chatter. The Buddhist monk Thich Nhat Hanh suggests:

Breathing in, I calm my body.
Breathing out, I smile.

It is very simple, very effective. As Christians, we may want something more biblical:

Breathing in, I draw your Spirit into my body,
Breathing out, I release my soul in joy.

It is important, however, that we not get too theological, so that we start filling our heads with all kinds of religious thoughts— this too would be an evasion of the present moment, of silence, and of listening. We may find that the Buddhist phrases, rooting us in our bodies and in a welcome to the present moment, prepare us for being Christian, for hearing the word of God, better than anything explicitly biblical.

We may all come in time to the point of being a little tired of the anxious, vain, indulgent selves we prop up every day by our inner noise—so tired in fact that we turn around toward a different way of being in the world. We discover a different way of being with others, a way not characterized by the constant negotiation and jockeying of selves in words, but a way characterized by humility and listening through silence. From the Desert Fathers we learn, "A brother who shared a lodging with other brothers (much as we do in our houses) asked Abba Bessarion, 'What should I do?' The old man replied, 'Keep silence and do not compare yourself with others.'"

One warning: when we make our first efforts at silence, we will discover just how much noise there is in our heads. This is part of the process, the initial sense of seeming impossibility. The sheer fact of trying to keep silence makes us consciously aware of how little silence we actually have, and how unable we are to listen. But if we persist, slowly and gently as the Spirit leads, we will discover the inner life calming and a deeper ability to hear and respond to the direct, joyful summons of God to new life in him.

⌒Healing for Others⌒

W HEN YOU ARE STILL NEW TO contemplative spiritual
practice, you are likely to regard the practices as things
you do for yourself, things to help you connect with God, things
to help you get through the day. As you progress, and as your
practice loses all its savor, you are likely to think that something
has gone wrong. At this point many people drop out or wander
off to a different teaching that, for a while, provides distraction,
a fix for the spiritual ego or the zest of novelty.

But if you stay with a practice long enough and so prove your
commitment, grace will bring to the surface all the unhealed
wounds and traumas in your life. As these wounds are healed
you will discover whole new possibilities for your life.

It is like you suddenly wake up from a nightmare and realize
there is a whole new way of being alive. And then the focus of
your spiritual and religious practice shifts away from yourself
to other people. You sense the urgency and immensity of God's
love for others and yearn to present these others to God, for
their happiness and for God's joy. Being spiritual is no longer
something you do for yourself. You no longer try to love others
because you think that's the way to be a good Christian. Instead,
you release yourself to the urgency of God's love that flows
through you for others. Stabilized by love, your life becomes
like an open frame through which God can give his love and
peace and healing to the world.

Christ Is Our Happiness

A T TIMES IT IS HELPFUL TO ASK OURSELVES where we are finding, or looking for, happiness. I mean happiness in the deepest sense of the word—in the sense of *makarios*, the Greek word that means not only happiness but blessedness. Makarios is the word used in the familiar Beatitudes of the Gospels: blessed, happy, are the poor in spirit. Where do we as contemplatives find our makarios? Or more precisely: In what do we become blessed and happy?

The Beatitudes suggest poverty of spirit, grief, injustice, hunger, thirst for righteousness and peace, and purity of heart as the places where true happiness is found. I don't think this means that we are to actively seek out poverty of spirit, or grief, or hunger, or persecution, as if they in themselves could be our happiness. Rather, Christ and Christ alone, as the light and life and love of the Godhead, is our happiness, and poverty, hunger, injustice, or grief can become the means of happiness when they force us to reach through them, beyond ourselves, for a new intimacy with Christ, a man of divine sorrow as well as joy. The more we grow in this intimacy, the more patterned and habitual it becomes for us to reach through unavoidable suffering for Christ's life and the more we begin to feel that our suffering is part of Christ's own redemptive work in the world. Our suffering takes on the meaning of Christ himself suffering in us. On a practical level, this means that we learn to practice mindfulness in difficult situations and letting go to God, accepting the unavoidable suffering, all as part of our commitment to remain one with Christ and what he has allowed in our lives.

We become makarios in Christ, the living Word of the Father. He and only he is our makarios, our happiness and blessedness. Even the relaxations we enjoy, or special days of celebration, when clung to apart from our devotion to Christ, become tedious and empty. This is something we learn only by experience. Our hearts were made for nothing less than union with God in love. Everything in this world was meant to be a sacrament, an outward sign through which that love is given and known. Thus everything everywhere has at least the potential to be the means of a communication of love between ourselves and God—a great inflowing of God and a release of ourselves. But when we cling to things as if in themselves they could make us happy, and we cut God out of the picture, we are left with the empty husk of reality, a sacrament emptied of its inner meaning.

In the end, we discover with St. Paul a kind of equanimity in good and bad circumstances, whether we have little or plenty (Philippians 4:11–12). This is because we are no longer searching to find our wholeness, our satisfaction, on the surface of things and events in the world, but have learned to reach through them as the outward forms for an exchange of love with Christ. This is our makarios, our happiness and blessedness, and is realized in something as simple as giving thanks for the good and pleasurable things in life and making interior acts of self-offering in the midst of difficulties.

Foundations for Contemplation: The Cardinal Virtues

I N ONE OF HIS LATER WRITINGS THOMAS MERTON TOLD of his growing awareness that the junior monks whom he was teaching and mentoring did not benefit much from complicated theologies or discussions of esoteric spiritual traditions. Rather, what they needed was an understanding of the basic virtues of the religious life and discernment on how to practice them. The monastery is not so much an academy of advanced work or esoteric novelty. It is a humble workshop where the tools of good works enumerated in Benedict's Rule are practiced.

Those called to intimacy with God are correct to claim with zeal that the whole purpose of their lives is to grow in contemplative presence before God and a contemplative manner of living. We can also say that we discover in this vocation a love and care of God that goes beyond all human understanding. And we understand that in this way of union with Christ we will be asked to accept what causes frustration and anger and sadness as the crucible in which a special kind of intimacy with our Crucified Lord is forged. These are the mysteries that course through the contemplative life: a dying and a rising, a great impoverishment in spirit and an unspeakable enrichment, a fracturing and a wholeness.

Yet for all these understandings, the foundation of the contemplative life is not laid in thinking great thoughts, having great insights, or having overwhelming experiences. Sometimes we might overemphasize the exalted life of contemplation without having first laid a foundation in the homely.

We lay the foundation for our union with God by practicing the most sensible and humble, commonplace virtues, once known as the cardinal virtues. These are prudence, moderation, justice, and courage. When we take care to live with other people by practicing these virtues, we find within our relationships the space and freedom to engage in the more theological virtues and the deeper mysteries of life. Temperance or moderation means not being greedy, not clinging to material possessions, physical or intellectual or spiritual pleasures. Justice means honesty and not using others as means to our own self-centered ends. It means regarding others as having something of God in them, and honoring that. It thus implies humility and modesty. Courage means being able to stay committed to relationships, vocations, or avocations for the long haul, being able to suffer the pains that lead to depth, maturity, and wisdom. It is patient and long-suffering. Prudence means being skilled, in spiritual as in practical matters, at choosing the most balanced and appropriate course for long-term growth. It means, more often than not, taking things slow and steady when we want to pitch ourselves forward.

Moderation, justice, courage, and prudence are the foundations for making a human being human. They are the humble tools by which we apply ourselves in the workshop of daily life. Only in so far as we are human can we be available to God.

Contemplation
and Action in One Love

As the contemplative life blossoms in us, we naturally find unexpected sweetness and delight in solitude. Our hearts are drawn out into a wordless knowing and being known by God that seems to defy all language.

The interior life demands its tithe of our time and energy; God is calling us urgently into ourselves so that we can leave our selves behind. "My beloved . . . the lonely wooded valleys," wrote John of the Cross in a kind of poetic exultation of this experience, "the strange islands, the resounding rivers." We may have come to know what he means by this point in our journey. The lonely wooded valleys and strange islands and resounding rivers are the solitary places in our own hearts. They are our opening to the divine life.

This kind of contemplative experience can overwhelm us. It can seem to speak more directly to our hearts than the common obligations of daily life. Worshiping together with other Christians can feel loud and garish by comparison. We may find ourselves actually looking down on other Christians or resenting the intrusion of others into our day!

All such looking down, taking offense, and resentment at active duties points to an imperfection. It means that our hearts, naturally enjoying the good things of God, are yet selfishly attached to them. Our growth in the contemplative way means to live surrendered in this tension between where our hearts are naturally drawn and the rest of our lives. It is good to remember the great St. Teresa of Avila telling her nuns that exalted states of prayer were wonderful, but they still had to do the dishes and mop the floors!

Of all the medieval spiritual teachers, the little-know Flemish mystic John of Ruusbroec can be of greatest help to us. John's basic point was that to be united to God meant to live and flow in God's own life. John looked at the Christian doctrine of the Trinity, which often seems so remote from ordinary life, and he saw something amazing. He saw that God was neither simply contemplative stillness nor simply outward, redemptive activity. Rather, he saw God as a life of pulsating love. This love draws everything back into itself in total unity, and then bursts forth in creativity and the multiplicity of creation.[8] God the Father flows out of himself into God and Son and the Holy Spirit. Such is the love and joy in the Trinity that this bursts forth in the vast multiplicity of creation. But then the opposite movement, the ebbing back to unity, takes over. The Holy Spirit, secretly working in creation, in human hearts, begins to draw creatures to Jesus Christ as the true Word of God. United with Christ we are then drawn back through him into wordless contemplative union with God the Father. The practical lesson that John drew from this for us is this: if we want to live a life of union with God, we have to simultaneously develop our ability to flow with both parts in God's life. We are drawn by the indwelling Spirit into a loving union with Christ, which leads through the heart of Christ into a wordless, contemplative simplicity and unity in God. But then, the same love that drew us into this unity impels us outward into a creative engagement with the world, carrying God's loving call, and God's Spirit into the world.

For us to truly live in God, our contemplative solitude and prayer turns into an active, bright-eyed engagement with creation, language, the church, and our communities. Both the ebbing into union and the flowing into action are one life of Love, the divine life, being lived out in us.

Every Day Is for Union

E VERY DAY WE WAKE UP FROM SLEEP,
        go about our lives
            sometimes with success, sometimes failure,
            sometimes anguished, sometimes relaxed,
                and then we go back to sleep again.

And every day the still, small voice,
        that calls us to love and honesty and presence
            is speaking there in the innermost chamber of our souls,
            waiting for us to awaken to its presence.

This voice can lead us through our day quietly,
        without fuss,
        without protestation,
        without show—
            lead us to live our day as an act of fidelity to the love
                that is not only in us
                but is drawing all of humanity into itself.

If we are to hear this voice
        we will have to listen for it
        and this means learning
            to listen past
                our chattering consciousness,
                the legion of anxious, distressed, compulsive voices.

In our silent prayer we take up the practice
  of quietly laying aside
    our self-obsessive inner monologue,
    that terrible need to narrate and re-narrate
     our lives.

    We do this so that we can hear the voice of One
      who speaks beyond all time
      and through all time
        and whose speaking calls our life into being.

This One who is beyond and with
  speaks the simplest truth: I am.

 I am bliss
   and I rejoice in you.
   And you are because I want you to be.
    Come and enjoy my love.

All the disciplines of the spiritual life,
  the methods,
  the practices,
  the religious beliefs,
    if they are not animated from our quiet listening
     to the voice that is other than our own,
     will become more godless
     until there is nothing left in them but our false selves
     living from one alarm to the next.

but if we listen to that voice, that voice that is not our own,
    that is so quiet and small,
        and if we devote each day to following that contemplative gift,
    everything can be drawn into God.

Our baptismal vows, our marriage vows, our monastic vows
    all can be ways
        of opening ourselves to the mystery that is completely Other
    and yet is completely one.

Over and over again Blessed Julian of Norwich gives us this one message:
    that God rejoices in us.

That divine rejoicing is right there, right here,
and the whole contemplative journey into humility is learning
    how to claim this
    and enter in
        as our only home, knowing that
            without this, wherever we might be,
                we are in exile.

There really is not much to our lives,
nothing all that very exciting:
every day we wake up from our sleep,
    go about our day
        with success, sometimes failure,
        anguished, sometimes relaxed,
            and then we go back to sleep again,

    and yet this most unspectacular day
        can be the means of our surrender to God,
        our union with God's rejoicing.

Saints Mary and Clare: Icons of Contemplation

I N LATE SUMMER OF EVERY YEAR the church celebrates two feasts that speak to the contemplative vocation. On August 11, we celebrate the feast of Saint Clare of Assisi, companion to Saint Francis and founder of the contemplative community of Poor Clare nuns. On August 15, there is the Feast of the Assumption of Mary into heaven, known in the Orthodox Church as the feast of her Dormition—literally, her falling asleep in Christ.

St. Clare represents the monastic ideals of poverty and prayer leading to powerful, feminine wisdom in God. Clare is a woman who stripped her life down to its bare essentials, and in that bare poverty experienced the God who is all graciousness and gift. It was Clare, empowered by her experience of God's love, who consoled the embittered and dying St. Francis, healing him of emotional pain caused by troubles in his society.

We are to begin living our vocation every day, with love for the concrete realities and limitations of this life that we already have. We are to love our fellow human beings as they are given to us and in love for God. This love is not a sentimental dreaminess, but a well-defined and strong commitment to human reconciliation with God. It aims always at restoration of human dignity and transformation in grace. Love of this sort, and a life given to do "something beautiful for God," is what gives birth to real monastic discipline as we see in St. Clare. It is what animates authentic contemplative spirituality, not as resentment or a longing to withdraw, but with a desire for the well-being of all.

St. Mary's Assumption or Dormition is also an image of the contemplative ideal. In our contemplative prayer, our lectio, or during times we set apart for silent presence, we pass like Mary into a state of peace not unlike falling asleep. We enter the "wakeful sleep" of inward presence to the divine.

These two summer feasts remind us of our call to prayer and that the meaning of our prayer is love for God and for our neighbor. If our contemplative lives are true, they do not spring from resentment or a self-righteous disgust of the world. Such self-righteous disgust disguised as spirituality usually means that we have been hurt by the world or the church and are still living in the mode of hitting back resentfully at what has hurt us. Even though our contemplative practice will lead us to withdraw periodically from society, and will demand that we stop exposing ourselves to the violent, dehumanizing, and distracting entertainments of our culture, these turnings aside are authentic only when they are a turning toward God and our neighbors for love.

Contemplation
and Bodily Death

A S AUTUMN APPROACHES, WE ARE REMINDED that death is a part of all life. As William Shakespeare wrote in his seventy-third sonnet, "When yellow leaves, or none, or few do hang / Upon those boughs which shake against the cold." In the cycle of the monastery's worshiping life, this connection between autumn and death is highlighted by two feasts that take place on November 1 and November 2. November 1 is All Saints Day, when we celebrate the saints of the church, those who lived exemplary lives of grace and who we consider already taken up into joy in God. All Souls Day is a day when we pray for all those who have died, praying for their final movement into rest and peace in God. All Souls Day is thus often colored by grief and awareness of friends and family who have died— the great multitude of loved ones who have passed on before us. As we are in the chapel, singing the solemn chants for All Souls, the first chill winds of winter are blowing dried leaves from the trees across the monastery lawn. These feasts help us to live consciously with the reality of our dying and to claim it as part of our life with God.

Of course, we all experience death and most of us experience it many times in life before the Beloved invites us over that threshold. Yet there seems to be very little in our religious or secular culture to help us understand and appreciate the experience of dying in ourselves and others. The contemplative, who has consciously chosen to give her whole life in responsive love for God, is in a unique position to know the spiritual reality of bodily death and to hold open its deeper meaning for others.

Contemplative conversion is in itself a kind of death and a preparation for dying well. It recognizes the futility of the ego's search for fulfillment in created realities. Contemplative life is energized by the possibility of surrendering our ego-defined reality to be taken up into a participatory union with God. Thus the contemplative turns away from ego-centered cravings, obsessions, and moods in order to yield herself ever more fully to a life that transcends this world and yet aims to be directly present in every atom and moment. As Christians we say this is offering ourselves to the Holy Spirit to be made one with God in Jesus. The contemplative has turned away from trying to find satisfaction in earthly life, to opening to the Eternal Joy and Eternal Desire of God.

Some years ago, a sister named Scholastica Marie died of liver cancer, and we had the enormous gift of caring for her in the last few months of her often painful journey. She was a spiritually powerful and insightful woman—the first person to join our founder in his creation of the order. She became the mother of the community, whose love held us together. We in turn loved her immensely. Because of that love, we experienced her dying with a strange mixture of feelings. On one level there was the deep grief of losing a much-loved friend, with all the levels of numbness, denial, anger, and sadness. No matter how far we develop in the spiritual life, these reactions happen and it is foolishness and potential disaster to disallow or deny them. But at the same time, as we cared for Scholastica in her dying and then lived through her absence after her death, we also experienced a heavenly realm opening up all around her. Her cell, in which she died, became a place of immense spiritual light and peace. And in a sense, as contemplative monks and nuns, we already knew this realm, and already knew it as our true home. Having in part already died spiritually and turned to God, we were able to travel with Scholastica at least part of the way over the threshold of her death. There was a sense of light, joy, expansiveness, freedom, and truth. Dying is the most liminal, thin place we can experience.

Observing this great mix of feelings and experiences and at home in them, the contemplative is able to help others make sense of what they are experiencing. She is aware of how others may be opened to God in dying and can help them navigate the strange new worlds opening before them. She is already at home in the light that shines through death and can help others come to terms with their losses and grief and to accept the enormous gift being offered them through the door opened so briefly.

⸻ *Manual Laborers in Christ* ⸻

T HE MOST REVEALING ASPECT OF GOD that Julian of Norwich experienced in her *Revelations of Divine Love* was the amazing homeliness of God's love. God was not distant or cool, but immediately and completely present to her in great friendliness and simplicity, taking care of her in the most physical and humbling of human needs.

> For the goodness of God is the highest prayer and it comes down to the lowliest part of our need. It vitalizes our soul and brings it to life and makes it grow in grace and virtue. It is nearest us in nature and readiest in grace. . . . A man goes upright and the food of his body is sealed as in a purse full fair; and when it is time of his necessity, it is opened and sealed again full honestly. And that it is He who does this is shown there where He says that He comes down to us, to the lowest part of our need. For He does not despise what He has created, and He does not disdain to serve us even at the simplest duty that is proper to our body in nature, because of the love of our soul which He has made in His own likeness. (*Lesson,* Chapter 6)

For those drawn to seek God in prayer, no attribute of God could be more natural, attractive, or appealing than God's homeliness—God's simplicity, friendliness, self-forgetful care, and a total lack of pretense. Accepting this homeliness as part of our vocation in Christ allows us, as homely contemplatives, to meet an essential need in the life of the Church.

An art museum will need a general manager, building and landscape architects, show and program designers, public relations specialists, docents, and of course artists to produce artwork for the shows. But it will also have people, unseen and unheralded, who take care of the heating and plumbing, who trim the bushes, polish the floors. Likewise in the Church there are thousands of people already involved in designing, creating, and managing programs, people who are very much in the public eye. There are great preachers and leaders and administrators of all sorts. But churches also need an unheralded core of people who will tend to the bare basics, the underground structures of the spiritual life. The manual labor of the spiritual life is performed by homely contemplatives who risk the stripping away of worldly goods and conventions and every variety of external grandiosity as part of a radical encounter with God. The Church will always need people who will go into that place where the programs, glamour, and arguments must all fall away—where words themselves, let alone doctrines, cease to have substance. These are people whose calling is to live to a radical degree of exposure and openness to God's loving.

We are opened, in all the fragile complexity of our being, to the love of God, and we learn to be unconcerned about ourselves, just as God does not worry too much about the divine dignity. Just as manual laborers in the art museum take care of the grime of a building so that others may be nourished in its beauty and richness, so manual laborers of the spiritual life willingly walk into divestment so that others may be clothed. We enter into poverty of spirit so that others might be rich.

Once we except this call into hidden ministry, we would do well to follow Mother Julian's consistent admonition that we live into our vocation not with a grueling, agonizing intensity, but with lightness and limpidity of spirit. Our most essential witness to the Church and the world is to reveal that the place of spiritual poverty, where all the exciting glamour of being church is stripped away, is not a place of anguish and darkness, but of light and strange freedom. This is our gift for the Church.

⌐Silence and Communion ⌐

WHEN PEOPLE TALK TO ME ABOUT JOINING the monastic community, they often ask me about the depth of friendship between the monks and nuns. They see how we work together, pray together, eat together, and recreate together but they also feel the silence of the monastery and observe how the members relish solitude. Understandably, they want to know if there are deep friendships, and if so, how they happen.

I always find this question difficult to answer, because while I and others experience a profound spiritual intimacy in the community, this intimacy comes about almost indirectly, unconsciously, out of a shared, lifelong commitment to prayer. The intimacy is not something we try to make happen in the community. Most of us have a preference for solitude as the place where we most easily step into our authentic selves before God. There are, moreover, periods of painful loneliness in the life. But over time, over the long haul, bonds of love, care, and mutual knowing slowly emerge until we wake up one day and realize that other people's lives have been so intricately inter-woven with our own that it would be impossible to separate the lives out from one another. Underneath the interpersonal tensions, underneath disagreements and bouts of loneliness, and woven through the silence, there is a depth of union and mutual presence to the mystery of others that is breathtaking.

This way of building community, through silence, prayer, and shared commitment flows out of our experience of God in contemplative prayer and meditation. Many of us are here because we discovered that, if we wanted anything at all to do with God, we had to allow ourselves to be drawn, as by an ineluctable tide, out beyond words into an ocean of silent presence. We discovered in the silence of contemplative prayer a manner of giving and receiving love that is beyond words, that is the opening of the heart, a whole and simple presence of soul. The abyss of the human heart cries out to the abyss of God. We discovered a way of knowing not mediated through words or ideas or images but is sheer presence in which we know and are known.

I don't think anyone has ever decided to take this experience of contemplative prayer and consciously tried to apply it to community. Again, communal intimacy is not something that we have to engineer. But just living the life, and learning how to love in the contemplative way, and practicing faithfulness to the community life day in and day out, our personal realities naturally begin to shift and we start relating to others, without thinking, without making a point or program out of it, from that place of presence. It is part of the long-term fruition of the life, and a foreshadowing of the heavenly kingdom.

I entered the community as a know-it-all college dropout and completely naive twenty-year-old. Joining me in my novice year was a new sister in her fifties, Oxford-educated, married once but now divorced, who had lived an academic life in Europe and the United States. We both were, and still are, strong-minded people with opinions that often diverge. But this sister and I share something that is at the center of our lives, yet is something that we can't even talk about because it goes clean beyond words—the contemplative experience of God in which there is nothing at all to point to, nothing on which a word can land. We simply know that about each other, and know that, after nearly two decades in the commmunity together, we have grown into that silence together. With this kind of union, separation or death has little meaning. This sister has become part of who I am at a most intimate level—without either of us trying for anything.

Putting Prayer
to Work at Work

I N A BUSINESS OFFICE SOME TIME AGO, I saw a sign posted on the wall that read, "Minimum Speed: 100 mph." I was pained on seeing this. Here was an office where people were pushed to go as fast as they possibly could. From other items posted on the walls I understood that they were also pushed into competition with each other, each striving to out-sell the other, even while they tried to be courteous and helpful to their clients. This kind of work environment is prevalent in our culture, even in our churches. We are encouraged to see ourselves as heroes engaged in a great conflict, as athletes and warriors fighting our way to victory. It is all about competition.

If we look at ourselves closely, we will see that the false self actually loves this sort of thing. It is turned on by it, stimulated and energized by competition, conflict, and struggle—as long as the prospects for victory look good. But if the false self loses, it gets grouchy, resentful, hateful, and angry, or just delusional. Think of Arthur Miller's play *Death of a Salesman*. The main character, an elderly salesman, has not been nearly as successful in life as he had dreamed of being. But because his whole self-worth is tied up in the dream of business success, he is forced to live in a fantasy world where he can pretend to be great. This alienates him from others in a haze of unreality and leads finally to his suicide. For many alive today, it is either the "thrill of victory" or the "agony of defeat."

To be a Christian means to have died to this idea of life as heroic conflict or a drive toward self-realization in earthly things. Being baptized means that we leave this view of life behind like an old set of clothes in order to dedicate ourselves to our Lord and his work in the world, surrendered to his beautiful will and receiving the fullness of life directly from him. In practice this does not mean simply drifting off into a haze of irresponsible piety. It still means hard work and trying to do the best job possible. Indeed, many people already have work that is directly meaningful from a Christian point of view. Looking at their work, they can see how they are helping people, or building community, or providing resources that promote human flourishing. In this case, they engage fully in their work, pursuing excellence as an act of their devotion to Christ who has called them into their endeavor, and they make their work a subject of conversation and discernment in prayer.

Some of us, however, may have work that, for the moment, seems to provide no value except to keep a roof over our heads and food on the table, but we can engage this work with an aspiration to excellence simply because such aspiration, and the discipline it requires, will help us to grow as human beings and make us more useful to God in the rest of our lives. In short, the aspiration to excellence is still there, but the sense of our identity hanging on our success or failure is not. We have taken up our work as a response of love to Christ, and if we fail in the eyes of the world, we are still whole in Christ. This is what allows us to do the best possible job we can do, yet not to overwork, and to rejoice when someone else does a better job, or beats us to the prize. Our work is not about us; it is about the common goal of human flourishing that demands the aspiration to excellence, and if someone else "wins" the prize, we share in their victory. Christians are at once totally committed to excellence in this world and human flourishing, and totally freed from having their identity or self-worth hang on individual success. If we go 100 mph, it's because we have decided that, at this time, it's needed. But even as we speed along, our hearts are not set on arriving, but on the Christ who is already with us.

⟶ FOR EVERY SEASON

A COUPLE OF YEARS AGO, I ASKED our monastic community to take up one spiritual practice each week: mindful breathing when using the computer one week, then mindful eating, mindful turning on and off of lights, mindful interruption of negative thoughts, as you will see in this final section of *Words for Silence*. For our monks and nuns, this was less an imposition of a new regime, and more an invitation to be curious and explore how a more recollected, less distracted life might feel.

These meditations are for every time of the year, every season, and every place. If we have lived a whole day without once being aware of our breathing, I would guess we have not really lived at all. If we have gone a day without inviting ourselves to smile and be present, we have done nothing more than survive.

Wherever we are, in whatever state we are, if we call ourselves back to our sense of the present moment, here and now, and we smile, we have entered the kingdom of God. Prayer is then something we embody, transparent to God in the present moment and alive with God's own life.

⌐ Surviving Panic ⌐

WHEN I FIRST CAME TO THE MONASTERY I was under the impression that the spiritual life was a matter of heroic self-sacrifice leading to union with God. I had the grim view, gained from a limited reading of the more challenging saints, that there was no prospect for spiritual reward or consolation for seeking God or trying to love him. It looked to me like a lifelong climb up a mountain of broken stones with no peak ever to be reached. Yet I felt in my inmost being that climbing that mountain was the only real possibility for me.

My view at the present is not so grim—not because I have discovered all kinds of spiritual favors, but because the mountain—or more correctly, the story of my life as the climbing of a mountain—has been taken away from me. God has asked me to live with less and less of a dramatic story. I have discovered that the mountain was something I needed at that time to give me a story that was heroic. It was also something I put there to save me from panic.

When the story of our lives—the one that we've created for ourselves—no longer makes sense, we almost always panic and immediately begin generating a new one. But the mystics point us to another possibility, what they often call the "way-less way." As long as we continue living in time, we will always feel like characters in a story, a story that says, "Last year I was there, and now I am here, and next year I could be there." But the way-less way points us to a different kind of consciousness in which there is very little "I" making a trek through time, and the present moment takes on much more importance.

Mindfulness and conscious breathing, for those called to live with less of a narrative, are almost survival techniques. Practicing them is like growing a set of lungs after having been tossed out of the miasmal pond onto the frightfully sunlit, hard land. Mindfulness and conscious breathing help us to learn that it is OK to let go of the ego's concern for itself in a grand story, and stripped of this narrative, to stand in the present moment where God is, receiving and responding in a new kind of freedom.

⌒ Joy through Self-Denial ⌒

WHEN WE TALK ABOUT SELF-DENIAL, we are not talking about knocking ourselves down with pleasure in our own suffering. This is the image we often have of self-denial, and it is based in violence. I suggest instead that authentic self-denial is the entirely peaceful and liberating experience of letting go of our anxious self-concern and inviting God's life into us. Doing this allows our true self, eternally real in Christ, to emerge.

As we have seen earlier in this book, Julian would say that what we today call the "false self" is based in wrath. By wrath, Julian means a fundamental refusal, rejection, or opposition to reality itself. We all have this because we are all sinners. But this does not excuse it.

So what does denying such a wrathful false self mean? Clearly it cannot mean trying to impose cheerfulness on ourselves. Such top-down demands on our emotional life would be just another manifestation of the false self's wrath and violence. Rather, denial of this false self begins with a deep and compassionate vision for just how much suffering we are causing to ourselves and everyone by remaining in our old state. We look into our wrathfulness, our negativity in whatever form it lives in us, and we see that fundamentally it does no good. Not creatively changing a situation, it only makes us and others suffer more. If we look very deeply into this low-level wrathfulness and feel its tension in our bodies, we will likely see that it is based either on fear or grief. We are then getting at the real emotional root underneath our complaining and negativity. And once we are at this level, it becomes possible to choose to let go of the wrath, to let it flow out from us. I experience this most viscerally in my body as a kind of unknotting of negative energy in my belly that then flows out with my breath. This letting go of low-level wrath is a kind of dying in ourselves; it feels like a deflation, a surrender. The second step is then to make the conscious choice, a little prayer, to invite God's life and light into ourselves. I experience this again as an in-breath that draws God's glad light into my lungs and belly and the whole of my body. This yielding of ourselves to God's life, a life that, initially at least, feels quite foreign to us, is the essence of the Christian contemplative way.

As Julian tells us, many things are opposed to God, but God is not opposed to anything. This is the revelation given to us in blazing clarity in the person of Jesus Christ. Many people were opposed to Jesus, they even killed him. But Jesus loved those who hated him. He was opposed to no one. Thus in inviting God's life into our own, we are yielding ourselves to a life that is strange and foreign to the "wrathful contrariness" that is the baseline reality of our false selves. We are making the choice to turn and yield ourselves to what is unlike ourselves.

What practical steps can we take toward such a love for God that invites this strange new life into us? I am going to suggest a specific practice that is the most powerful way I know of inviting God's life into my own, turning away from my anxious self-concern and yielding myself to the divine joy. Fifteen years ago I would have scorned this practice as facile and ten years ago I would have questioned its theology. But all my doubts have been removed by steady personal experience of the discipline. It is the practice of mindful breathing—and is really the core monastic practice of recollection.

In mindful breathing, we follow our physical breath, in and out, as our doorway to the present moment. Only by being in the present moment can we invite God's life into ourselves. The best way to be mindful of our breath is to say a short prayer as we breathe in and out. It goes like this:

Breathing in, I welcome your calm into my body.
Breathing out, I smile.

Breathing in, I dwell in the present moment.
Breathing out, I know this is a wonderful moment.

Those of you familiar with Thich Nhat Hanh will be familiar with this way of mindful breathing. I learned it from him. But even though I have adapted it from Buddhist sources, we need have no fear about being less Christian by adopting this practice. Breathing mindfully sets the stage for the Christian gospel. How are we possibly to love God and our neighbor unless we are calm in our body and able to smile and welcome others in the present moment? If we are lost in the fraught anxiety of our false selves that is basically conflictual, unable to smile, and mentally distracted, we will not be able to offer any real service to others. Moreover, in practicing this kind of breathing prayer, we are inviting God's strange life into us, giving the Spirit room to breathe in us.

For this week I invite you to simply begin a new life of self-denial with me—self-denial not as a war against yourself, but by mindful breathing that invites God's life into your own. You can do this when waiting anywhere, walking to the mailbox, driving, sitting at table, calming yourself down after a painful incident or a hard period of work. It can be done everywhere. It is so refreshing to pray with our bodies and our whole selves!

And lest we think calming and smiling is facile, we can remember that Julian says, "It is the most honor to Him of anything that we can do, that we live in our penance gladly and merrily because of His love, for He looks upon us so tenderly that He sees all our living here to be penance" (*Lesson*, Chapter 81).

Breathing in, I welcome your calm into my body.
Breathing out, I smile.

Breathing in, I dwell in the present moment.
Breathing out, I know this is a wonderful moment.

Putting on Christ
with Our Garments

THOMAS MERTON, IN A SERIES OF ESSAYS called *The Inner Experience,* wrote this late in his life:

> The worst thing that can happen to a person who is already divided up into a dozen different compartments is to seal off yet another compartment and tell him that this one is more important than all the others and that he must henceforth exercise a special care in keeping it separate from them. That is what tends to happen when contemplation is unwisely thrust without warning upon the bewilderment and distraction of Western man. . . . The first thing that you have to do, before you start thinking about such a thing as contemplation, is to try to recover your basic natural unity, to reintegrate your compartmentalized being into a coordinated and simple whole, and learn to live as a unified person. This means that you have to bring back together the fragments of your distracted existence so that when you say "I" there is really someone present to support the pronoun that you have uttered.[9]

Later in the same series Merton wrote: "Anyone who is already divided against himself, and at war with himself, had better get himself together before he sets out to conquer the realm of ascetic meditation and contemplative prayer. Otherwise the divisions already present in him will tear him apart in short order."[10]

I feel led to offer mindful breathing to everyone seeking a contemplative life or a deepening of the lived experience of union with God. I offer it not so much as a way of prayer (though it could be that), but more as a preparation for prayer and meditation. Mindful breathing is, to use Merton's terms, simply a way of reintegrating a distracted and fragmented life into a coordinated and simple whole so that we are able to be human again, and so able to celebrate Eucharist or to pray the Rosary or practice prayer healthily and with our whole selves. It is especially helpful in a culture where we tend to rush too quickly and aggressively into spirituality and contemplative prayer to our own detriment.

Now, I would like to apply this practice to our getting dressed every morning. Before we put on each article of clothing, we can stop and recollect ourselves in our bodies:

Breathing in, I welcome your calm into my body.
Breathing out, I smile.

Say this once for your shirt, once for pants, once for belt, socks, shoes. It will take you a couple extra minutes to get dressed, but what you gain—a centeredness and reminder of who you are as you start your day, is an amazing gift. Having welcomed God's presence into your body, you are free to be at God's service for the rest of the day.

If we are already distracted by the time we get dressed in the morning (and most of us are already locking into anxiety and mental obsessiveness from the moment we wake up!), we will be unable to honor the presence of God in the opening of our day and the preparing of ourselves to do God's work. We will have missed once again that very, very special gift of God in our lives.

Instead of charging angrily into our day or cringing at its approach, we can greet each day as another opening of our lives to God's life. We approach our day with the peace of Christ and with a smile. Only with this peace and the openness, presence, and self-mastery communicated by the smile are we able to receive the gift of each morning. It is like being given the freshness and hope and joy of our original baptism, our loving espousal to God and death to all that takes us away from God.

Breaking Cycles of Negation

I N OUR THIRD MEDITATION ON RECOLLECTION through conscious breathing, I think we can begin to appreciate that what we are doing is learning how to interrupt the self-reinforcing feedback cycle of our inner selves. In a previous mediation, I introduced this as a way of self-denial. We can now see that such self-denial means:

First, we become aware of our interior moods and cycles. This means not being lost in them and identified with them.

Second, because of our calling and mission in life, we take adult responsibility for our inner reality. Having a strong and clear vision of what we are about gives us a reason to apply ourselves to spiritual practice.

Third, we stop ourselves periodically to invite God's life, a life different from our own, into ourselves. Julian says that we are not always in peace and love, but that God in peace and love is always working in us. In our practice, we thus consciously invite the divine peace and love to expand outward from our essence (Julian's metaphor!) into our thoughts, emotions, and bodies. This is mature. This is caring. This is enormously healthy. It is a work of love that enables us to love.

For this meditation, I would like to shine the light of awareness on our tendency to get angry, anxious, frustrated, or in any way negative inside ourselves. Once we start paying attention, we will realize this is happening all the time, from annoyance with the alarm clock ringing in the morning to anger with the wadded up pillow as we go to bed! But the moment we catch ourselves slipping into a destructive cycle, we can stop whatever we are doing for the love of God and open the whole cycle to God with our breath. I will remind you of the basics:

Breathing in, I welcome your calm into my body.
Breathing out, I smile.

Breathing in, I dwell in the present moment.
Breathing out, I know this is a wonderful moment.

We can add a couplet to our prayer in times when we find ourselves especially caught in painful inner states:

Breathing in, I accept that there is this pain.
Breathing out, I give it to you in love.

Then we can go back to the beginning and continue by welcoming God's calm into our body, and recalling ourselves to this moment as the wonderful moment of Christ's presence. It is very important to go back to the beginning until there is inner freedom. Sometimes all we need is one repetition. Sometimes we will need a dozen. However many times we go around the cycle, we are making the choice to be conscious of the pain we are experiencing, to dis-identify from it, and to open ourselves to God.

There is nothing self-contradictory in saying that the moment is wonderful even when pain is present. In fact, we will feel the pain and frustration more sharply if we affirm the moment. The inner tantrum may really explode when we try to dis-identify with it! This is why we have to be courageous. Such a moment of courageous awareness—naming something instead of being sucked into identity with its negative energy—is wonderful because grace is then bringing us to a place of adult responsibility. We are learning to open the inner movement of our hearts to God for healing.

⌒ Feeding Christ as We Eat ⌒

F OR THIS MEDITATION, I WOULD LIKE TO TURN our awareness
to something very concrete: our eating. Three or more
times a day we take nourishment into ourselves. We can be
totally oblivious to the gift of our food, and our interconnection
and interdependence with all of life—with the earth and all of
the cosmos—through our food. When we stuff our food down,
trying to fill an emptiness in ourselves, we are oblivious to its
gift. We are behaving abusively toward the rest of this planet
that has given of itself to us. When we rhapsodize about special
delectations, and develop a haughty culture of high cuisine, we
are missing the gift. When we allow our negative feelings and
obsessive thoughts to invade the meal, we also become oblivious
to the gift of food, because we are not aware in joy of what we
are eating.

Eating can be an act of deep acceptance of ourselves as bodily
creatures. This is humility. Eating can also be a recognition of
our dependency on the life of this planet. This too is humility.
When we eat even the simplest meal, we take into ourselves
the sun, the rain, and the soil, the green shimmering leaves,
and glowing clouds. And because our union with Christ is not
merely a mental, ethical, or emotional reality, but is based in
the transfusion of our physical bodies by his risen Glory, when
we eat we are integrating this whole planet's mineral, vegetable,
and animal life into the risen body within us.

We can also experience eating as the tender loving of God
for us, as a foretaste of the love that will raise us in transformed

bodies at the Resurrection. All of this is being offered as we sit down to raisin bran, or a casserole, or an egg. Think of how, when we eat a tuna casserole, we are taking the whole salty life of the oceans into ourselves in the tuna! And the whole life of the ocean is made over to Christ through us. And how, through the life of the ocean, its huge waves and teaming schools of fish, God is tenderly loving and supporting us in our bodily life. This is a marvelous thing.

We can make a happy, pleasurable meditation at every meal to help us eat in the marvelous mystery of love and care that food is. We can begin the meal with our now familiar phrase:

Breathing in, I invite your calm into my body.
Breathing out, I smile.

This will call us back from our thoughts to be truly present to the gift of the food we are about to eat. We can even put our fork down if we find ourselves distracted and return to the present moment with our familiar prayer. Then, as we eat, we can pay attention to the fact we are eating and say inwardly:

Chewing, I taste the goodness of God.
Swallowing, I feed the life of Christ in me.

The Not So Great
or Terrible Oz

MOST OF US WILL REMEMBER THE SCENE from *The Wizard of Oz* in which "Oz the Great and Terrible" is revealed to be an illusion produced by a bumbling and anxious man behind a curtain, pulling levers and pushing buttons. He had kept the whole world in thrall by fakery, by a projection of great terribleness.

I can't think of a better image for what Thomas Merton famously called our false selves. On the outside there is a projection of greatness. It may be great terribleness, or it may be great charm or accomplishment or talent, but whatever form the greatness takes, it is meant as an exhibition of power. It is meant to keep other people away, or to control other people, or to create a drama or conflict that allows me to remain at the center of a social setting. But behind a curtain somewhere there is a deep-seated fear pulling all the levers and pushing all the buttons. The most difficult thing to realize is how much and how thoroughly we fool ourselves; not only do other people think we are Oz the great and terrible, but we think so too!

For this meditation, I invite you to be conscious of yourself whenever you are slipping into "Oz the Great and Terrible" mode. This is whenever a feeling of conflict, anger, or contentiousness rises up within you; whenever you are possessed by thoughts or moods or desires or dreams; whenever you are thick inside, tumultuous, or feeling huge. Whenever you feel this way, step back, look at yourself calmly and say, "Oz!" In saying that one word, you are claiming a true awareness of your false self, you are seeing the powerful illusion that wants to sweep you and others into its energy. And you also see the craven fear that is making the pyrotechnics happen behind the curtains. Seeing all this, you can smile and say, "Oz."

This can be very hard to do. There are times when we desperately yearn to be enraged or carried away in some high mood. This mood makes us feel invulnerable, safe, and big. To look at it and say, "Oz," drains it all of any power, a power we very much crave.

In offering the image of "Oz the Great and Terrible," I hope to give you a tool for a little more leverage over your false self. Discover the power of the smile in dissolving what appears to be life-threatening drama. The drama isn't even there anymore.

Breathing in, I calm my body.
Breathing out, I smile.

Breathing in, I see the great and terrible false self.
Breathing out, I smile at it.

Breathing in, I see the fear pulling the levers.
Breathing out, I smile.

All of this is done for Jesus. There are, after all, two things that Oz the great and terrible cannot do. He cannot be real, and he cannot pray. In letting the whole "Oz-self" fall away, we discover our natural being, our soul's essence in Julian's terms, where we are already praying, already one with God. This is the great simplicity that is our natural state and the core of our being.

⟶ *Darkness and Light* ⟵

OUR DAILY, CONTEMPLATIVE WORK with conscious breathing, mindfulness, and short prayers is a powerful way of actively seeking God and preparing ourselves for grace. When we stop in our day to breathe the peace of God deeply into ourselves and to smile at the present moment, we are interrupting the monologue of the false self in order to open and yield ourselves to God, who is already here and now. This is precisely the work of self-mortification that is most necessary in the contemplative life—not hair shirts and fasting, but learning to dis-identify with the anxious obsessions in our hearts and minds that we have wrongly thought of as ourselves.

To put it more simply: in our practice of mindful breathing we are learning to take ourselves less seriously, and to create some space around the psychodrama of our lives. Through that space, that gap, grace gets in.

Another simple yet demanding contemplative practice is to pause and call yourself back to mindfulness each time that you turn on or off an ordinary light. Every time we turn on a light, we can stop and say:

O God, you make my darkness bright.

Every time we turn off a light we can stop for a moment to say:

O God, darkness and light to you are both alike.

In this practice, which is simple and powerful, we call ourselves out of our fears and aims several times a day. We interrupt the anxious inner monologue that is not who we really are; we step back and practice offering ourselves to God and rejoicing in the Light that God is.

And lest this sound too childish, too simple, we can recall what spiritual teachers have been telling us from time immemorial: It is useless for us to make all kinds of verbal protestations about the contemplative life and our search for union, and at the same time refuse to do anything, no matter how small, in the middle of our day, to gain a little freedom from ourselves. No matter how eloquent our theology, how deeply felt our spirituality, how sophisticated our culture, if we cannot summon the energy to work at these little tasks of mortification we will never be free from the tyranny of ourselves and never be free enough to rest in God.

Unknown Errors
of Type One

C OMPUTERS PLAY A LARGE PART IN THE LIVES of most people in the developed world. Even a contemplative nun may do a good deal of her daily work at a computer. Because personal computers are such a new phenomena—the PC came into being only a generation ago—there has not been much reflection on spiritual intention and practice in our use of computers. There is even a very odd, widespread sense that our computer use falls outside of the realm of spiritual practice, mindfulness, and humility—that how we behave with computers is not really relevant to our spiritual lives.

Our practices of mindfulness show us that time with a computer can be full of heaven. Heaven can be right here and now as we write a blog or lay out a church bulletin. Even the failure of our intentions can be heavenly. The application can freeze up, the hard drive can fail, and the printer refuse to join our network—and all that can be a part of heaven. It's a question of the attitude we bring. Many of us will remember an error message that used to pop up on older computers and which has the ring of a Zen koan to it: "An unknown error of Type One has occurred." Then the little fizzing-bomb icon would appear and you would have to restart the computer, perhaps losing a good deal of work.

If we look closely at our experience of working on the computer, it is easy to see why so much negative emotion and stress are generated in our use of them. What is it about computers that they seem to elicit the most infantile and negative emotions in us?

For our contemplative practice, being mindfully aware when we use our computers is very important. Any experience of frustration with them is a red flag that tells us that we are using them in the wrong way—hoping to achieve ourselves through them, or rushing in a way that demonstrates a lack of mindfulness. Fixing these problems does not come from getting a newer, faster computer. It will come from a change in interior disposition. We can actually work at a computer amazed and grateful for what it is able to do.

When you sit down to work, mindfully recollect yourself by paying attention to your breath and reciting:

Breathing in, I calm my body.
Breathing out, I smile.

Breathing in, I dwell in the present moment.
Breathing out, I know this is the moment of Christ.

Then, before working, recall yourself to your vocation in God, again following your breathing:

Breathing in, I know that you have called me to this work.
Breathing out, I yield myself to you in joy.

When we grow frustrated or find ourselves hunched furiously over the keyboard, pounding the keys or thwacking away on the mouse, we can realize that we have lost our freedom. At those times, we need to stop, take a breath, and recall ourselves to God again. Perhaps we need to go get a drink of water or walk out to the mailbox, before we can return healthily to our work. The point is to live consciously and release your ego: "An unknown error of Type One has occurred." Thanks be to God.

⟶ Our Natural State Is Union ⟶

To a Visitation Sister who was troubled by her impulsiveness and lack of recollection, St. Francis de Sales wrote:

> Accustom yourself to speak rather gently, to walk slowly, to do everything quietly and in moderation; you will see that in three or four years you will have regulated your impetuosity. And remember to act and speak in this gentle manner on those occasions where you are not pushed by your impetuosity and where there is no apparent reason to fear it, as for example, when you are going to bed, getting up, sitting down, eating; in short, don't excuse yourself [from this practice] at any time or anywhere.[11]

I love St. Francis because he is so quiet and gentle about the spiritual life, and yet very insistent upon practices that gradually yield us to God. The practice of interior discipline and watching our bodily comportment as well as our moods and inclinations was so important for Francis because he believed that such practices allow us to become open and responsive to God.

I love how he suggests this most demanding spiritual practice of bodily recollection to the troubled Sister and says that "in three or four years" she will see some results. Is it worth it to work at something for three or four years?

For Francis it was. And for any of us, we only have two choices: remain stuck in our anxious, shy, or domineering egoism—an egoism that causes pain to ourselves and to others; or become gradually transparent to God, able to bring the gospel to others through the manner of our presence. It is a question of what you want in life. Ask yourself: What do I want? Do I want more of myself, or more of God?

Even so, it may take years to begin to see results.

For this final meditation, I would like to refresh the most basic teaching. This is to take time throughout the day, whenever we have to wait, whenever we are called to a new activity, whenever we feel conflicted, whenever we are interrupted, whenever we are tired or distracted, to recite a short prayer as we consciously breathe in and out:

Breathing in, I welcome your calm into my body.
Breathing out, I smile.

Breathing in, I dwell in the present moment.
Breathing out, I know this is a wonderful moment.

We may wish to rephrase the last line as,

Breathing out, I know this is the moment of Christ.

No matter how far we get in our practice, there is no leaving this behind. You may have all kinds of thoughts about spirituality and prayer, about your inner self or about relationships, about your vocation and mission, and if you don't have this simple awareness in your body, your whole self, then you will never develop a contemplative approach to life. Mindfulness is the foundation for all other practices.

Blessed Mother Julian tells us our soul's essence is held by God in a natural state of simplicity, peace, and blessing. In our essence we are *already* completely open and transparent to God, so much so that we cannot tell where God ends and we begin. That is her teaching and arises from her experience. She even says that God "wills that we believe that we experience Him constantly (although we imagine that it is but little) and by this belief He causes us evermore to gain grace" (*Lesson*, Chapter 10). As we become freer, more open, less driven by fear and pride, we are able more and more to let ourselves go to this reality. We are content to be just this.

Breathing in, I welcome your calm into my body.
Breathing out, I smile.

Breathing in, I dwell in the present moment.
Breathing out, I know this is the moment of Christ.

⌒NOTES

1. All references to Julian's *Revelations of Divine Love* are to the edition by Fr. John-Julian Swanson, OJN, entitled *A Lesson of Love* (Lincoln, NE: Universe, 2003). In-the-text references take this form: (*Lesson*, Chapter—). Users of other editions of *Revelations of Divine Love* should note that the page numbers will be different.

2. References to St. John of the Cross's works are to *The Collected Works of St. John of the Cross*, translated by Kieran Kavanaugh, OCD, and Otilio Rodriguez, OCD (Washington, DC: ICS Publications, 1991). In the text, references will refer to the title, book, chapter, and paragraph number (*Dark Night*, I.2.3), or title, stanza, and paragraph number (*Spiritual Canticle*, 3.2).

3. John Cassian, *The Institutes*, translated and annotated by Boniface Ramsey, OP, in Ancient Christian Writers series no. 58 (New York: The Newman Press, 2000). In-the-text references will be to book and chapter number (Eight.III).

4. The best description I know of these practices in terms of contemplative prayer is a practice called "The Welcoming Prayer" in Cynthia Bourgeault's *Centering Prayer and Inner Awakening* (Lanham, MD: Cowley Publications, 2004), 135ff.

5. The writings of the Vietnamese Buddhist monk Thic Nhat Hanh have been helpful to many people.

6. Richard Wilbur, *New and Collected Poems* (New York: Harcourt Brace Jovanovich, 1989), 187.

7. Thomas Merton as quoted in Annie Dillard, *Pilgrim at Tinker Creek* (New York: Harper and Row, 1988), 268.

8. For a standard edition of John Ruusbroec's work see *John Ruusbroec: The Spiritual Espousals, The Sparkling Stones, and Other Works*, translated by John Wiseman (Mahwah, NJ: Paulist Press, 1986). For an excellent introduction see Louis Dupre, *The Common Life: The Origins of Trinitarian Mysticism and Its Development by Jan Ruusbroec* (New York: Crossroads, 1984).

9. *The Inner Experience* is an unpublished manuscript that was presented as a series of essays in *Cistercian Studies Quarterly*. This passage is from the first page of Essay I, "Notes on Contemplation" (vol. 18, 1, 1983).

10. *The Inner Experience*, Essay VI, "Some Dangers in Contemplation" (vol. 19, 2, 1984).

11. Francis de Sales and Jane de Chantal, *Letters of Spiritual Direction*: Letter #1064, Classics of Western Spirituality series (Mahwah, NJ: Paulist Press, 1988), 164.

About Paraclete Press

Who We Are

Paraclete Press is an ecumenical publisher of books and recordings on Christian spirituality. Our publishing represents a full expression of Christian belief and practice—from Catholic to Evangelical, from Protestant to Orthodox.

Paraclete Press is the publishing arm of the Community of Jesus, an ecumenical monastic community in the Benedictine tradition. As such, we are uniquely positioned in the marketplace without connection to a large corporation and with informal relationships to many branches and denominations of faith.

We like it best when people buy our books from booksellers, our partners in successfully reaching as wide an audience as possible.

What We Are Doing

Books

Paraclete Press publishes books that show the richness and depth of what it means to be Christian. Although Benedictine spirituality is at the heart of all that we do, we publish books that reflect the Christian experience across many cultures, time periods, and houses of worship.

We publish books that nourish the vibrant life of the church and its people—books about spiritual practice, formation, history, ideas, and customs.

We have several different series of books within Paraclete Press, including the bestselling Living Library series of modernized classic texts; A Voice from the Monastery— giving voice to men and women monastics about what it means to live a spiritual life today; award-winning literary faith fiction; and books that explore Judaism and Islam and discover how these faiths inform Christian thought and practice.

Recordings

From Gregorian chant to contemporary American choral works, our music recordings celebrate the richness of sacred choral music through the centuries. Paraclete is proud to distribute the recordings of the internationally acclaimed choir Gloriæ Dei Cantores, who have been praised for their "rapt and fathomless spiritual intensity" by *American Record Guide,* and the Gloriæ Dei Cantores Schola, which specializes in the study and performance of Gregorian chant. Paraclete is also the exclusive North American distributor of the recordings of the Monastic Choir of St. Peter's Abbey in Solesmes, France, long considered to be a leading authority on Gregorian chant performance.

Learn more about us at our Web site:
www.paracletepress.com,
or call us toll-free at 1-800-451-5006.

Other Contemplative Titles from Paraclete...

Ponder These Things
Rowan Williams

ISBN: 978-1-55725-509-9
$16.95, Hardcover

Ponder These Things invites readers to explore and reflect on the depths of meaning in three classic icons of the Virgin and her Child from the Eastern Christian tradition. Icons have been described as "theology in line and color" and, in tracing the movement within these icons, the Archbishop of Canterbury discovers the pattern of love that they reveal, a love that invites and embraces us so that we no longer remain as spectators, but find ourselves caught up in the drama that unfolds itself before us.

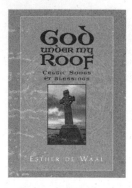

God Under My Roof
Esther de Waal

ISBN: 978-1-55725-516-7
$14.95, Hardcover

From birth to death, from dawn to dusk, from the dark of winter to the light of midsummer, for the Celtic peoples praying was part of the pattern of life. The prayers of household and farm and workplace were handed down from generation to generation in oral tradition.

Esther de Waal has brought together some of the most significant of these poems, blessings, prayers, and songs that enable us to touch the vivid sense of the presence of God that marks Celtic spirituality.